HEALING

from ABUSE

HOW THE ATONEMENT OF JESUS CHRIST
CAN HEAL BROKEN HEARTS
AND BROKEN LIVES

HEALING
from ABUSE

JANENE BAADSGAARD

CFI, AN IMPRINT OF CEDAR FORT, INC.
SPRINGVILLE, UTAH

ISBN 13: 978-1-4621-1032-2

Published by CFI, an imprint of Cedar Fort, Inc.
2373 W. 700 S., Springville, UT 84663
Distributed by Cedar Fort, Inc., www.cedarfort.com

LIBRARY OF CONGRESS CATALOGING-IN-PUBLICATION DATA

Baadsgaard, Janene Wolsey, author.
Healing from abuse : how the atonement of Jesus Christ can heal broken lives and broken hearts / Janene Baadsgaard.
    pages cm
ISBN 978-1-4621-1032-2
1. Abused women--Rehabilitation. 2. Abused children--Rehabilitation. 3. Abused men--Rehabilitation. 4. Psychological abuse--Religious aspects--Christianity. 5. Church of Jesus Christ of Latter-day Saints--Doctrines. I. Title.

BV4596.A2B33 2012
261.8'327--dc23

                    2012007510

Cover design by Angela D. Olsen
Cover design © 2012 by Lyle Mortimer
Edited and typeset by Michelle Stoll

Printed in the United States of America

10 9 8 7 6 5 4 3 2 1

Printed on acid-free paper

For my family

Contents

Contents

Introduction

I've been a professional journalist writing about family issues for three decades in newspapers, magazines, and books. Because my life's work has been to inform and uplift families, I've been on a continual search for the latest research and have interviewed numerous professionals in an effort to gather and share information with my readers. My career has placed me in the unique position to receive many letters, emails, and phone calls from readers all over the world. The most deeply poignant questions and heartbreaking experiences I've received concern destructive relationships. While I don't claim to be an expert, I'd like to share a select sample of these true stories of courage and recovery, along with some important information and insights I've collected on this most difficult topic.

Our hearts can be broken for various reasons, but perhaps one of the most devastating wounds is inflicted when we are betrayed by those we trust or abused by those we love. There is a way to untangle ourselves from the web of destructive relationships without losing our capacity to trust and to love. The Atonement of Jesus Christ is the only way to leave human cruelty behind and become the son or daughter of God we were meant to be.

We often speak about the fact that the Atonement provides a way for us to repent of our sins. What is often left unsaid is that the Atonement is designed to heal us from all the effects of sin—both those we commit and those committed against us. Healing from abuse and betrayal is a personal journey we take with the companionship of our Savior, for the Atonement also heals a broken heart. "He healeth the broken heart and bindeth up their wounds" (Psalms 147:3).

Whatever type of abuse we've experienced, the injury to our soul requires divine healing. There is a light and power that will guide us through all the pain we experience in this life so we can move into the future unburdened with the past. That power and light is Jesus Christ. No matter what has happened to us, the Savior knows where to find us and how to heal us.

We don't like to talk about abuse or betrayal. It is easier to pretend it doesn't exist—but it does. Those who have been injured need information, understanding, and support. If you are or have been caught in the web of a destructive relationship, there is something better for you. There is light, joy, and peace available to every son and daughter of God. Each of us deserves to be treated with dignity, kindness, and respect.

Destructive relationships are the source of great pain. Those who have been abused or betrayed know how it feels when every part of their body and soul aches with an inner sadness far deeper than any physical injury or illness. They know what it feels like to be cheated, humiliated, demeaned, beaten, stalked, violated, betrayed, treated unfairly, lied to, placed in mortal danger, neglected, controlled, abandoned, blackmailed, or threatened. There is no excuse for abuse; excuses keep us stuck in a web of damaging associations. We can get unstuck.

Abuse is evil—against both civil and moral law—and it has to stop. In order to fulfill our potential, we need regular contact with healthy people who treat us with respect. We need a solid understanding of what is right and what is wrong. We need education about destructive relationships and how to respond. We also need an accurate view of the part we play in the abuse cycle.

In this book we'll focus on how to recognize and stop abuse, examining and overcoming the effects of destructive relationships, and how to heal and move forward. In many cases, an abuser is never going to admit guilt. Family members or friends may not be helpful in the healing process. This book is designed to help survivors of cruel relationships heal with or without a confession from the abuser or validation or support from others.

Time does not heal the wounds of abuse; only the Savior can. Each person who has been treated with contempt deserves a divinely given view of themselves and others. As we draw near to Christ, we will learn how to create a safe and loving environment for ourselves. As we receive the ennobling gifts of the Atonement, we will come to know who we really are and how we and others deserve to be treated. With our Creator's unconditional love and Christ's infinite gift, each of us can experience the peace and love that surpasses understanding and the exquisite joy that is the right of every son or daughter of God.

NOTE: The English language is sometimes awkward in its use of third-person singular pronouns. Sometimes I have referred to both the abuser and the victim as "he or she," while at other times, for simplicity's sake, I have chosen one or the other. I do not mean to imply that an abuser should be viewed as primarily male or the victim as primarily female—or vice versa. Both abusers and victims are all too commonly found in both genders.

Section One

HOW TO RECOGNIZE ABUSE

Chapter One

WHAT ARE ABUSE AND NEGLECT?

We are all involved in a variety of relationships and are continually confronted with difficult issues based on gender, disposition, opinion, and personality. While these differences are difficult, the majority of these issues can be resolved with mutual tolerance and respect. Abusive relationships are different. Each of us is a beloved son or daughter of God, and no one has the right to demean, frighten, or threaten us or to verbally, physically, or sexually assault us. If we have been harmed in these ways, we have been abused and must act now to stop it.

We can't stop what we don't understand or acknowledge; awareness is half the battle. What follows is a discussion for those who desire to eliminate all destructive relationships from their lives. These definitions aren't the most detailed or definitive available. I'm not placing myself in the role of a professional. This discussion is meant to increase awareness so we no longer minimize, dismiss, or justify our own or others' abusive behavior.

Most people assume they already know what abuse is and don't need a definition. The fact is, many victims do not fully understand what constitutes abuse, and most don't know they have the right to set healthy personal boundaries in all relationships. Many victims are especially confused about how to handle abuse situations in the family. Thus defining abuse is a vital place to begin our discussion.

DEFINING ABUSE

Abuse is any action or failure to act that damages the sense of worth, well-being, development, dignity, growth, or safety of another human being. Abuse is cruel behavior or the failure to stop cruel behavior that causes nonaccidental injury or trauma. Injury or trauma can occur when something bad happens to us (abuse) or when something good like love, respect, protection, and nurturing does not happen (neglect). Neglect is the intentional or unintentional failure to meet the basic needs of someone who is dependent on others for those needs to be met. Neglect is a passive form of abuse and includes the conscious and repeated failure to provide the goods, services, time, and attention to meet someone's physical, emotional, intellectual, and social needs, as well as protection, education, and positive reinforcement.

Abuse is the nonaccidental use of unnecessary or excessive intimidation or punishment that results in physical harm, pain, or mental anguish. It is a pattern of behavior used to establish power and control over another through fear, threats, and coercion. It is an attack on the soul that harms body, mind, and spirit. Abuse controls, threatens, hurts, damages, grieves, diminishes, frightens, ignores, oppresses, exploits, or harms another human being. Those who abuse knowingly use power or influence over someone for selfish motives. Abuse by omission is allowing someone else to harm or injure an individual without doing anything to intervene or stop the abuse.

A short list of abusive behavior includes violent anger such as yelling, cursing, hitting, kicking, biting, choking, or burning; forced or manipulated sexual activities either outside or inside marriage; verbal assaults such as belittling, name-calling, or constant criticism; controlling behavior such as a required accounting for every penny spent, isolation from family and friends, or withholding affection; exploitation such as exposure to patently inappropriate movies, jokes, language, magazines, or Internet material; threats such as saying or doing things that cause others to feel anxiety or fear; pious superiority such as causing others to feel worthless, unloved, or condemned through intimidation, domination, or control; and neglect such as lack of medical care or the fulfillment of other physical and emotional needs. For a more comprehensive list of abusive behavior, see the Appendix.

We tend to think of abuse as something that lands the victim in the hospital and the abuser in jail. Yet most abuse is difficult to prove, not physically obvious, and seldom known to anyone outside the relationship. Whether the abuse is physical, verbal, emotional, mental, religious, or sexual, it causes the victim to feel confusion, powerlessness, pain, sadness, and grief. Victims feel degraded, betrayed, unloved, vulnerable, invisible, afraid, angry, and depressed. They want the pain to stop, but they don't know what to do. It is important to understand the abuse cycle, because cruel behavior will not stop until victims hold their abusers accountable for their behavior.

THE ABUSE CYCLE

The abuse cycle can be thought of as a clock, where the hands go around and around but never stop. The cycle includes the following stages:

Tension building. A feeling of pressure may occur suddenly or build over a period of time. The victim is aware of the increasing tension and tries to please, pacify, or humor the abuser.

Abuse occurs. Abuse may be triggered by minor or major incidents. Apologizing to or trying to reason with the offender does not stop abuse.

Honeymoon period. Remorse is expressed by the offender following the abuse. This is the period when the offender may vow to change by giving gifts, making efforts to pacify, or acting as though no mistreatment occurred.

Neutral phase. This is when the abuser is sure the offended will not tell. Gifts or apologies end. Normal behavior resumes. Tension starts building again.

If we choose to stay trapped in the abuse cycle, we also choose the consequences for both ourselves and our children. When adults abuse other adults, the victim has some power to defend herself and leave the relationship. Adults who abuse children, who cannot defend themselves or leave the relationship, must be stopped by other caring adults. When Jesus said, "Behold your little ones" (3 Nephi 17:23), among other things he wanted us to understand the importance, beauty, and innocence of children and the power adults have over them to harm or heal. The consequences are also clear: "But whoso shall offend one of these little ones . . . , it were better for him that a millstone were hanged about his neck, and that he were drowned in the depth of the sea" (Matthew 18:6).

President Thomas S. Monson affirmed the Church's stand on abuse when he said,

> Some children witness their fathers savagely beating their mothers, while others are on the receiving end of such abuse. What cowardice, what depravity, what shame! Local hospitals everywhere receive these little ones, bruised and battered, accompanied by bald-faced lies that the child 'ran into the door' or 'fell down the stairs.' Liars, bullies who abuse children, they will one day reap the whirlwind of their foul deeds. The quiet, the hurt, the offended child victim of abuse, and at times incest, must receive help. A district judge, in a letter to me, declared: 'Sexual abuse of children is one of the most depraved, destructive, and demoralizing crimes in civilized society. There is an alarming increase of reported physical, psychological, and sexual abuse of children. Our courts are becoming inundated with this repulsive behavior.' The Church does not condone such heinous and vile conduct. Rather, we condemn in the harshest of terms such treatment of God's precious children. Let the child be rescued, nurtured, loved, and healed. Let the offender be brought to justice, to accountability, for his or her actions and receive professional treatment to curtail such wicked and devilish conduct. When you and I know of such conduct and fail to take action to eradicate it, we become part of the problem. We share part of the guilt. We experience part of the punishment.[1]

EXCUSING ABUSE

Abusers always excuse their behavior. As long as victims accept these excuses or promises not to re-offend, nothing will change, and the abuse will continue. Some abusers excuse their actions by referring to their behavior as justified or necessary. In truth, victims never cause abuse. Cruel behavior is a choice an abuser makes.

Abusers do not believe that others deserve to be treated with kindness and respect. They seldom acknowledge that their behavior is wrong, and they lack the desire or commitment to change. Deviant, cruel, or controlling behavior gets them what they want and accomplishes their purposes. Abusers don't feel the pain they're causing and do not care about the impact of their behavior on those around them. Some abusers admit they have a bad temper or strong impulses but lie to themselves and others when they claim they're powerless to control their actions. For example, an abuser can control her anger at work, school, or church and then come home and use the slightest provocation to "blow up" at a spouse, child, or sibling.

Most abusers can effectively manage their behavior, anger, and impulses when they have something to lose. They don't abuse people outside the family or above them in work or church hierarchy because they know they would be prosecuted, fired, or excommunicated. They carefully choose when and where to abuse—behind closed doors at home or privately at work or during church activities where their actions are hidden and they are safe because family members or associates are unwilling to hold them accountable for their behavior.

It's never right to hurt someone. Abusers may claim reasons for what they do, but those reasons never provide an adequate excuse. Excuses don't free us or others from inevitable consequences. When we fully understand that there are no excuses for destructive actions and words, we will better learn to hold ourselves and others accountable for abusive behavior.

FOLLOWING COUNSEL

President Gordon B. Hinckley gave this warning to men who abuse their wives, but it holds for women as well:

> Some [men and women] put on a fine face before the world during the day and come home in the evening, set aside their self-discipline, and on the slightest provocation fly into outbursts of anger. No man who engages in such evil and unbecoming behavior is worthy of the priesthood of God. No man who so conducts himself is worthy of the privileges of the house of the Lord. I regret that there are some men undeserving of the love of their wives and children. There are children who fear their fathers, and wives who fear their husbands. If there be any such men within the hearing of my voice, as a servant of the Lord I rebuke you and call you to repentance. Discipline yourselves. Master your temper. Most of the things that

make you angry are of very small consequence. And what a terrible price you are paying for your anger. Ask the Lord to forgive you. Ask your wife to forgive you. Apologize to your children.[2]

President Hinckley further counseled us about the nature of our conversations when he said: "We seldom get into trouble when we speak softly. It is only when we raise our voices that the sparks fly and tiny molehills become great mountains of contention. . . . The voice of heaven is a still small voice; likewise, the voice of domestic peace is a quiet voice."[3]

This advice does not mean husbands and wives never have different opinions. Elder Joe J. Christensen of the Seventy said: "Occasionally, we hear something like, 'Why, we have been married for fifty years, and we have never had a difference of opinion.' If that is literally the case, then one of the partners is overly dominated by the other or, as someone said, is a stranger to the truth. Any intelligent couple will have differences of opinion. Our challenge is to be sure that we know how to resolve them."[4]

RIGHTEOUS JUDGMENT

We've been counseled to "Judge not, that ye be not judged" (Matthew 7:1), which is often misinterpreted as meaning we should never judge. Yet learning to judge between good and evil is an important exercise of mortality. We can't make final judgments regarding another person; that is reserved to God. However, we are instructed, through the use of our moral agency, to make righteous judgments about actions or behavior.

Our motivation for judging is vital. We can't judge righteously if our motivation is revenge or evening a score. Righteous judgment is motivated by love. Though is seems contradictory, the most loving thing we can do for an abuser is to hold them accountable for their behavior. Removing ourselves from an abusive relationship is an act of love. Why? Because an abuser can't repent as long as we allow them to keep abusing us.

No one has the authority to deny the power of the Atonement to heal another, even the person who abused us. Righteously judging behavior as evil but suspending final judgment of an individual requires humility, discipleship, and consecration and is one of the ultimate forms of charity. Often we simply don't have all the facts and can't determine if someone's behavior is a sin or a mistake. Sin is willful disobedience to the laws of God we've received through the scriptures, the prophets, or the Spirit, whereas a mistake results from ignorance. Whether the abuse we suffered was a sin or a mistake, it has to stop, and the person responsible must still be held accountable.

ABUSE CAUSES CONFUSION

Human beings instinctively recoil from any cruelty; but if abuse is tolerated, victims soon become confused or numb to what is happening. Abuse by strangers is most troubling, but abuse by those who might have loved us is devastating. If a stranger degrades or threatens us, steals our innocence, or beats us up, we know we've been abused and have no trouble understanding that person is doing something wrong. We likewise have no trouble understanding that person should be held accountable for his cruel behavior in the courts of law and by the local Church leadership. Yet if our parent, spouse, sibling, church leader, coach, or teacher threatens or degrades us, steals our innocence, or assaults us, our reaction may be conflicted. Wanting so much to be loved, we tolerate abusive behavior, thinking we're being Christlike or forgiving. Victims want to believe that eventually the abuse will stop because abusers often apologize or promise to change. Because no one wants important relationships to fail or their reputations to be tarnished, abuse is often denied, tolerated, or hidden. Worse yet, abuse continues because the victim believes she deserves cruel treatment. If victims don't report destructive behavior to professionals outside the relationship, abuse will continue. If our efforts to stop abuse fail, we have no obligation to continue the relationship.

We are commanded to forgive our abusers, but we are not commanded to live with or associate with them. Those caught in the cycle of abuse often waste their lives trapped in a web of confusion, emptiness, self-deception, fear, loneliness, anger, isolation, and shame. Everyone involved in the cycle of abuse is accountable for their actions or failure to act. We must stop abuse now so we can move forward and develop into the loving sons and daughters of God we are meant to be.

ZERO TOLERANCE

Quoting from the Church Handbook of Instructions, President Gordon B. Hinckley said, "Abuse cannot be tolerated in any form."[5] Yet many of us do tolerate abuse in many subtle or less-than-subtle forms, or deny there is a problem. Whatever form it takes, abuse is wrong and flies in opposition to the teachings of Jesus Christ. "The Family: A Proclamation to the World" states, "We warn that individuals who violate covenants of chastity, who abuse spouse or offspring, or who fail to fulfill family responsibilities will one day stand accountable before God."[6]

The victim is never at fault—never. There is no excuse. It is time for all of us to wake up and become part of the solution to this pervasive and all-too-common problem. Abuse is an issue for everyone, whether we have experienced it or not; people who live with abuse are in pain, and they eventually turn that pain inward or outward. Much of what sickens our society is the direct result of abuse. It is up to us to save our children.

President Hinckley said:

> Children don't need beating. They need love and encouragement. They need fathers to whom they can look with respect rather than fear. Above all, they need example. . . . Save the children. Too many of them walk with pain and fear, in loneliness and despair. Children need sunlight. They need happiness. They need love and nurture. They need kindness and refreshment and affection. Every home, regardless of the cost of the house, can provide an environment of love which will be an environment of salvation.[7]

Those who are involved in destructive relationships must draft a personal declaration of independence from abuse. When victims change their behavior, the sick game is over. When victims stop tolerating abusive behavior from those around them, abusers can't continue to abuse without suffering the consequences. The battle of good and evil is real and worth our best effort. Saving the souls of men must start with our own.

NOTES

1. Thomas S. Monson, "Precious Children, a Gift from God," *Ensign*, June 2000, 6–7.
2. Gordon B. Hinckley, "Women of the Church," *Ensign*, Nov. 1996, 68.
3. Gordon B. Hinckley, "Except the Lord Build the House . . . ," *Ensign*, June 1971, 72.
4. Joe J. Christensen, "Marriage and the Great Plan of Happiness," *Ensign*, May 1995, 65.
5. Gordon B. Hinckley, "Personal Worthiness to Exercise the Priesthood," *Ensign*, May 2002, 54.
6. The Church of Jesus Christ of Latter-day Saints, "The Family: A Proclamation to the World," *Ensign*, Nov. 1995, 102.
7. Gordon B. Hinckley, "Save the Children," *Ensign*, Nov. 1994, 53–54.

Chapter Two

RECOGNIZING AN ABUSER

D o you think you can spot an abuser? Don't be so sure. Contrary to usual typecasting, abusers are not scary-looking people. Abusers come from every age group, culture, and socioeconomic group, and from both genders. Many abusers have sterling reputations and are the last people to be suspected of abuse. An abuser may serve in religious, civic, or business assignments with a high level of responsibility. They may be a friendly neighbor who invites our son over to watch a movie, or a brother-in-law who sleeps over at our house. An abuser may be a Scoutmaster, little league baseball coach, or drama teacher at high school, a boy or girl at the playground, or a supervisor at work. Statistically, however, most abusers are family members. Most abuse comes from spouses, parents, grandparents, or other caregivers, such as siblings, uncles, aunts, cousins, or other close acquaintances. We simply can't identify an abuser from outward appearance, family relationship, career title, or religious position.

CHARACTERISTICS OF ABUSERS

Those who treat others without respect and dignity have not come to terms with abuse in their own past or the devastating consequences of their behavior. Their character development is stuck. Abusers sacrifice others to preserve their distorted image of self. They deny their wrongdoing and project it on other people. They are unwilling to suffer the pain that follows significant self-examination. Personal growth requires that we see ourselves as we really are. Abusers despise the light of truth that exposes them and hate any person who penetrates their carefully crafted self-deception.

Some words or phrases that describe abusers include the following: controlling, two-faced, negative, deceitful, rigid, overbearing, hateful, pushy, petty, backstabbing, angry, gloomy, devious, unable to connect emotionally, determined to have their own way at any cost, self-absorbed, always right, destructive, excessively intolerant of criticism, confusing, bad-tempered, self-righteous, judgmental, and greedy. Abusers often display an egotistical sense of entitlement or superiority and attempt to escape guilt and suffering by robbing others of their self-worth, freedom, and dignity. Abusers use their power over others in subtle or obvious ways to avoid changing themselves.

Some abusers are more difficult to identify than other abusers because they are intellectually devious. They aren't motivated to be good but rather to appear good to others. They are keenly aware of social norms and committed to preserving their public image. They often attempt to appear ultrarighteous for the disguise it offers them. They live in fear that their pretense will be exposed to both themselves and others.

Most abusive behavior can be traced back to the childhood of the abuser. Yet becoming an abuser is a choice or a long series of choices. Abusers do not want to feel emotional pain, so they refuse to examine their true motives. They seldom, if ever, admit to the pain they inflict on others. Abusers refuse to face the overwhelming evidence that their actions (or failure to take action) have caused great damage to those around them. They are unwilling to suffer, but those around them suffer. Abusers eventually create a controlled but dysfunctional circle of family and associates. If victims remove themselves from the unhealthy relationship, abusers find new victims.

Abusers spend a lifetime attempting to hide from their own guilt. Rather than improving over time, their behavior gets worse as it becomes more and more difficult for them to go back to the beginning and admit they have been wrong all along. To do so would require that they face their self-deception and the harm they have caused themselves and others. So they run from the voice of their own conscience by playing the role of self-declared victim or by labeling, criticizing, controlling, and tearing down others.

They refuse to respect other points of view, lie or tell half-truths to confuse, withhold information, threaten, deny they did anything wrong, control, make false promises, take advantage, manipulate, and humiliate. Abusers lack basic empathy for others and view their victims as objects to achieve their purposes.

Rather than admitting that their rage or deviancy stems from their own choices, abusers place the blame for their behavior on their victims. In an effort to convince themselves and their victim that their actions are justified, abusers frequently launch into a synopsis of all the victim's faults or bring up past mistakes. However, regardless of the abuser's claims, the victim's behavior never justifies abuse. Claims that the victim "caused" the abuser to act a certain way or that they "deserved" the treatment they received are the abuser's way of maintaining control. Abusers will resort to whatever method necessary to retain control and often display a tenacious persistence to achieve the objective they have in mind, no matter how deviant, irrational, or cruel. The abuser will inflict injury of any kind and at any level necessary to control the victim. After the abusive episode ends, the abuser will change strategy, act as though nothing has happened, or apologize without sincerity.

Maintaining an appearance of normalcy is vital to the abuser's deception. So long as the abuser can preserve the illusion that his actions are necessary, his power over the victim will continue. The goal is control, and in order to retain it, abusers build a nearly impenetrable web of lies meant to deceive their victim and themselves.

Sexual abusers are often confusing and cunning. They may appear friendly and helpful or offer gifts and favors to groom their victims to trust them. Sexual abusers use their position of authority or the victim's innocence and desire to please or obey as a way to manipulate or coerce their prey into sexual activities. Some sexual predators confuse their victims by claiming their activities are acceptable or medically necessary. Many victims are threatened, while others are told they wanted the contact or that no one will believe them.

Sexual abusers are often protected by families who would rather hide abuse than deal with it. Authorities are not called, and statutes of limitations run out. Pressure is put on the victim by the abuser or other family members to let it go. Abuse victims are often threatened with nasty lawsuits. Too many families stick their heads in the sand rather than deal with sexual abuse issues in a timely manner. If the victim is rejected or dismissed after her attempts to report abuse, the betrayal happens all over again. Too often, the non-abusing spouse chooses not to acknowledge what is going on or blames the victim.

Some families believe they can handle sexual abuse issues quietly within the family circle. Everyone should understand that all sexual abuse issues must be handled by professionals outside the family. Studies suggest that sexual abusers will not alter their behavior without direct outside-the-family intervention. Quick action should be taken to prevent future victims.

Violent abusers threaten to injure themselves or others; they display cycling depression; show obsessive, jealous, and controlling behavior; possess weapons; destroy property; and isolate victims from extended family, friends, and neighbors. Violent abusers deny the harm they've done, transfer their guilt to the abused, or manipulate their victims with fear of abandonment or withdrawal of financial support or love. Joseph Smith received this insight into the abusive mind in Liberty Jail: "When we undertake to cover our sins, or to gratify our pride, our vain ambition, or to exercise control or dominion or compulsion upon the souls of the children of men, in any degree of unrighteousness, behold, the heavens withdraw themselves; the Spirit of the Lord is grieved" (D&C 121:37).

MAKING DIFFICULT CHOICES

All abuse has the same effect—it destroys everything good such as confidence, love, and trust. Reporting abuse or ending a destructive relationship is the first courageous step in the process to healing. One woman described her experience with abuse this way:

> I remember a doctor lecturing my mom for not bringing me into his office before my eardrum ruptured, causing permanent hearing loss. I didn't dare tell the doctor Mom hit me on that ear when I told her it hurt. I learned early to stuff my screams down deep where no one could hear. When I became an adult and Mom could no longer hit me on the outside, she'd make negative comments about my body or tell me demeaning things my siblings had said about me. When physical assaults, verbal abuse, and threats were no longer

effective, my parents and siblings moved to intimidation, blackmail, stalking, harassment, and threats to kill, injure, or sue me. I had to stop tolerating this behavior before I could draw near to my Savior and receive the blessings of the Atonement. When I did, I discovered I was a beloved daughter of God who deserved to be treated with love and kindness. As a child I didn't have the power to change my environment. As an adult, I do. I no longer allow family members to treat me without respect even if that means I can no longer associate with them. Letting my family go was the most difficult thing I've ever done because I have forgiven them and I will always love them. Yet now I see what a positive impact that decision has had on my life with my husband, children, and now grandchildren. I no longer live in constant fear, diminished self-worth, and the pain of unrequited devotion. Today my life is filled with meaningful service, a loving marriage and posterity, people who are capable of receiving and returning my love.

One man described the way he successfully untangled himself from an abusive childhood this way:

> When I was a child, my brother told me to scream when my father beat me. He said Dad would stop quicker. I couldn't do it. There was a part of me I knew Dad was determined to break so he could control me. I couldn't stop the pain of him breaking my body, but I wouldn't allow him to break my spirit. Before he beat me, I remember staring into my father's eyes with a voice inside saying, If you have to do this, go ahead. But I will not bow down to this. You will not break me even if you have to kill me. I left home feeling so angry and bitter. It was years before I returned to church because my father represented the church to me. I married a woman who loved me back into activity. I didn't know there was that much love in the world. After a lesson one Sunday on coming to Christ, I decided to take all my bitter and angry feelings to the Savior. It took a long time, but my Savior helped me let go of the pain. Even though my father never changed and I couldn't have a relationship with him, in time, I forgave him. Now I am at peace. I have been blessed with children and grandchildren who have been raised with love. I never take the love we have for each other for granted.

One woman told me her young son was sexually abused by an older child in their neighborhood while playing at the elementary school near their home. This woman said that because the perpetrator's family was in their ward and she was friends with his mother, she decided not to report or press charges. She swept the incident under the rug, hoping her son would forget. Years passed, and her son grew more and more troubled. After a difficult adolescence that included drug addictions, her son finally admitted in court-ordered counseling sessions that he was racked with overwhelming guilt and knew God hated him. The young man didn't feel worthy to go to church or on a mission because of those experiences. This woman later discovered the boy who abused her son went on to abuse others.

"I didn't understand how profoundly the incident affected him," this woman said. "My son needed to know what happened to him was a crime. He needed to be told he was an innocent victim and the abuser should have been held accountable. I allowed my son to live alone in his pain for a very long time. He interpreted my silence and failure to act as a sure sign he must be guilty of something so awful it had to be kept secret. The day my husband and I and our son walked into the police department arm in arm and reported the abuse was the day our lives began changing for the better."

A victim should never feel guilty when he takes the necessary steps to place an abuser in the legal system. It's never too late for victims to take action. It is not uncommon for victims to come to an understanding of the evil of abuse slowly. It is not uncommon to keep it secret. There is tremendous pressure to keep quiet. But the evil of abuse will continue for generations unless victims hold their abusers accountable. It may seem easier to hide reality in an attempt to escape pain or protect reputations, but hiding abuse virtually always guarantees that abuse will continue. Survivors of abuse must make sure they protect future victims.

Some who are abused believe they must forever accept destructive relationships if they love their abuser. The truth is, if we truly love the abuser, we won't allow the abuse to continue. The pattern of nice behavior followed by abuse and then the subsequent apology or pretense that nothing happened will continue unless the victim puts a stop to it. Each time we permit ourselves to be victimized, we allow an abuser to chip away a piece of our dignity until we doubt our worth and lack the will to change our circumstances. Before long, we get used to being treated in violent, demeaning, or callous ways. If we stay a victim long enough, we no longer see ourselves in reality as a beloved son or daughter of God. Sometimes victims of abuse make excuses, such as the following: "But she's my mom. I need my mom." "But he's the father of my children. My children need a father." "He's my dad. I can't get along without his financial help." "But she's my wife. What will the children do without her?" Making excuses like these keeps everyone stuck.

Just because someone is related to us doesn't mean we should allow ourselves or others to be victimized. In fact, allowing children to witness abuse will guarantee that the cycle will reach across time to haunt the lives of our posterity for generations. Victims need to untwist their distorted reality, which tells them that the abuser's behavior will magically get better someday. Victims must reclaim their personal power, refuse to remain in the victim role, and make choices that end the abuser's control over their lives. Real love doesn't hurt. Life will not get better until we take action to stop the abuse.

ABUSERS' EXCUSES

Abusers always use excuses. Victims must be able to see the lie in these excuses and refuse to accept them. Common excuses include the following:

> *Rationalization:* "It's the way I am." "It was done to me, and I'm all right."
> *Minimization:* "You push my buttons." "It was just a little touching."
> *Self-Deception:* "He deserved it." "She wanted the contact."
> *Denial or Deception:* "I never did it." "She is lying."
> *Threats:* "If you tell, I'll sue you." "If you tell, I'll kill myself."

Some people believe abusers have been held accountable for their actions if they admit the abuse and apologize to the victim. An abuser's accountability must also include the following:
- full confession to all the people they abused
- full confession to all members of their family
- full confession to their religious and legal authorities
- acceptance of all consequences set by moral and civil law
- willingness to repent and change

- willingness to get professional counseling
- willingness to obey all protective orders
- willingness to separate from the offended
- payment for all costs incurred as a result of the abuse

THERE IS ALWAYS HOPE

There is always hope and healing for both the abuser and the abused. It helps to remember that even the worst abuser was once an innocent child. President Boyd K. Packer said in his October 1995 conference address: "Save for the exception of the very few who defect to perdition, there is no habit, no addiction, no rebellion, no transgression, no apostasy, no crime exempted from the promise of complete forgiveness. That is the promise of the Atonement of Christ. How all can be repaired, we do not know. It may not all be accomplished in this life. We know from visions and visitations that the servants of the Lord continue the work of redemption beyond the veil."[1]

Both the abuser and the abused need the Atonement to heal. Our Savior offers healing to everyone. One woman described her life-changing moment of choice this way:

> I was alone in a hospital bathroom after giving birth. I stood up to go to the bathroom when suddenly, I broke into a cold sweat and everything went black. When I woke up I was lying on the cold floor with a shadowy figure standing over me screaming. In an unexpected flashback, a horrific abusive experience from my childhood burst through to my mind with such force and clarity it felt as though my body was literally re-experiencing the abuse. Even though I had reported the abuse and removed myself from a relationship with my abuser, the memories continued to haunt me. Then, just as suddenly, my awareness returned to the present and I was back in the hospital bathroom.
>
> "You're hemorrhaging," the nurse screamed as she pulled the emergency alarm.
>
> Then everything went black again. I don't know how long it was before I woke up. I remember regaining consciousness with my eyes still shut in the blackness, once again reliving the past abuse. I rolled to my side, folding into a fetal position, feeling penetratingly alone.

"Dear God, please help me," I plead.

At that precise moment, I heard a baby cry. I opened my eyes and saw a nervous nurse standing next to my bed holding my beautiful, hungry, newborn daughter.

"Do you feel strong enough to feed her?" the nurse apprehensively asked.

"Oh, yes," I answered, eagerly reaching my arms out to receive her.

As I wrapped my arms around my daughter, I knew God had answered my prayer. My newborn baby needed a mother who knew how to love her. I decided that nurturing my daughter would now be my focus. I understood I could choose to live in my dark past or embrace my promising present. I chose the present. I could choose despair over what had happened to me or I could choose gratitude for the new future that was ahead of me. I chose gratitude. I could choose to wallow in the depravity of my past or I could choose to deeply love myself, my husband, and my child. I chose love. It has been a long journey to leave the abuse in my past behind, but I am kind and patient with myself as I heal. For now I know I have a choice, and every day, with the help of God, I choose to go forward with gratitude and love.

Our Father in Heaven has provided a way for each of us to triumph over evil. There is no sin so awful that it makes repentance or healing impossible; there is no wound so deep that the Savior cannot heal. When we clearly see the influence of abuse in our lives and then choose another way, the power of the adversary is broken and God's purposes are fulfilled in our behalf. When we choose to leave destructive relationships behind, we have access to the healing power of the Atonement. Though abuse causes exquisite pain, there is a compensating joy waiting for those who take the necessary steps to stop the abuse in their lives and heal. As we consistently refuse to participate in destructive relationships we will be blessed with a clear mind, loving heart, hope for the future, and lasting peace.

NOTE

1. Boyd K. Packer, "The Brilliant Morning of Forgiveness," *Ensign*, Nov. 1995, 19–20.

Chapter Three

UNDERSTANDING DECEPTION

Any action, word, or behavior that causes a child of God to doubt his or her divine worth is a great lie. Those who are abused are cruelly lied to. When we knowingly or unknowingly accept these lies and allow others to treat us without dignity and respect, we gradually lose the ability to see ourselves the way our Father in Heaven sees us. In addition, we grossly underestimate our value and restrict our ability to see reality and feel inner peace and joy.

One woman described the moment when she discovered she had been lied to about her potential as a daughter of God this way:

> When I was a nineteen-year-old college student, I worked three jobs to pay for room, board, tuition, and fees. There were times when I didn't have enough money for food or the necessary books for my classes. One night my art teacher pulled me aside after my evening drawing class and asked me if I'd be interested in earning some extra money by becoming a model for the art department. I was excited about the prospects of earning a little cash doing something besides cleaning toilets, but I was confused.
>
> "Why?" I remember asking him. "Why would you ask me?"
>
> "You have a perfectly proportioned body," my teacher answered. "You wouldn't have to pose nude. All our models wear clothing."
>
> I told him I'd have to think about it. Frankly, I was totally shocked. I'd spent a lifetime being told I was ugly and fat and that no boy would ever want to marry me. I went home that night and locked myself in the bathroom. Then I timidly looked in the full-length mirror. I always wore clothes that were several sizes too big, trying to hide what I considered were all my flaws. Piece by piece, I took off the oversized thrift-store clothing and stared at myself in

the mirror. For the first time, I looked at my reflection in the glass objectively.

Could it be possible, I remember thinking, *that what I've been told and what I've always accepted as facts about myself are lies?*

Then I broke down and wept. That was the beginning of my education on the miracle and sacred beauty of my mortal body. I was just beginning to understand the miracle and sacred beauty of my immortal soul.

CULTURAL TABOOS THAT PROMOTE SILENCE

In many societies, there is a cultural taboo against discussing insider information that will embarrass or dishonor a dating partner, family member, employer, or church leader. Instead of calling cruel behavior wrong, removing themselves, and holding abusers accountable, victims often focus on maintaining an image of well-being or attempt to endlessly self-improve. Many work hard on maintaining appearances rather than admitting that negative behavior exists in their relationships. Courageously facing and dealing with the truth, no matter how ugly, is always easier in the long run than living in denial. There is no humiliation in humility. As we draw near to the Savior, we understand the worth of every single soul—including our own.

Both an abuser and a victim can be self-deceived. When we believe we or others deserve to be treated without respect, we are deceived. Both an abuser and a victim can have a hard heart. We have a hard heart when we seek to avoid pain. As we draw near to the Savior, we will feel pain but we will not feel it alone. When we receive the gifts of Atonement, we develop character and wisdom through the pain we experience.

Many who have been abused waste much of life undervaluing themselves, believing the lies they were told. When we draw near to our Savior, we can discern a lie more quickly, before it harms us. Abusers seek to control their victims by telling them they are worthless, undeserving of love, or never good enough. Each victim develops her own way of dealing with cruel relationships. Some develop chronic health problems. Others develop perfectionism, obsessive/compulsive tendencies, or anxiety and panic attacks. Some develop eating disorders or become addicted to drugs. Others become depressed, emotionally disconnected, or overly pious. The only healthy way to deal with a lie is to see it for what it is and refuse to believe it.

VICTIM EXCUSES

As adults, we are accountable for the abuse we tolerate in our sphere of influence. Phrases like "He's not that bad" or "She just needed to vent" are often used as excuses for behavior that is unacceptable. Though most excuses are sincere, they are the result of confused thinking about love, forgiveness, patience, humility, hope, loyalty, and accountability. Many who have been abused may be deceived about the worth of their own souls.

Typical victim excuses include the following:

- If I (keep trying, love this person unconditionally, forgive him, get her the right counselor, get him the right medication), eventually this person will stop hurting me.
- If I were more (patient, humble, full of hope, forgiving, smart, organized, attractive), this wouldn't happen and this person would treat me better.
- I shouldn't talk about the bad things that have happened in my (childhood, marriage, or workplace) because I'm suppose to (forgive, honor my parents, keep my job, be more patient or longsuffering, keep families together).
- I chose to marry this person, which means I brought this situation on myself, so I have to (deal with this behavior because of my marital vows, keep our marital difficulties private, accept blame for choosing this person).
- My (dating partner, spouse, parent, sibling, or boss) has a (strong need to control, bad temper, uncontrollable addiction). To keep (the peace, my employment) I have to (go along with everything, tolerate her dominating/controlling ways).
- I've resigned myself to the fact that (dating relationships, work environments, marriage/family life) is supposed to be difficult and painful because (it's normal, that's the way it was in the family I grew up in, people don't change, this is my lot in life, nothing I do ever seems to improve anything, I don't know if I'll ever find anything better).

- When someone harms me I should keep it secret to (demonstrate my love or loyalty, keep our family together, maintain a reputation, ease embarrassment, stay employed, make sure everyone thinks highly of me).
- This person (is mentally ill, is an addict, doesn't know better, was abused as a child) and therefore can't be held accountable for their behavior.
- I have to keep abuse secret because (I don't want my dating partner/family member thought of this way, I don't want people to think of me this way, it will just stir up more pain, no one will believe me, it really wasn't that bad, my abuser will lie and make me look like the problem, take custody of the children, sue me).
- I have to stay in this cruel relationship because I don't really believe that I deserve better, and besides, this person is my (boss, husband, wife, mother, father, brother, sister, uncle, aunt, cousin, son, daughter, girlfriend or boyfriend).
- I can't end this relationship because (I'll lose my job, this person will kill themselves, go to jail, kill me, hurt me or the children) if I leave.

When we are self-deceived, we feel powerless. We live with constant fear and anxiety. In truth, we are not powerless. God will bless us with the courage to do the right thing, no matter how hard it is for us, if we ask for His help. "He giveth power to the faint; and to them that have no might he increaseth strength" (Isaiah 40:29). We cannot live the abundant life Christ promised if we are racked with guilt and fear. "I am come that they might have life, and that they might have it more abundantly" (John 10:10). When we join forces with the powers of heaven, we draw on a strength that far exceeds our own, and we are never alone. "If God be for us, who can be against us?" (Romans 8:31).

UNDERSTANDING SHAME

When survivors of abuse keep abusive behavior secret, they absorb the shame and guilt the abuser refuses to feel. Guilt is the feeling that you did something wrong, while shame is the feeling that you are something wrong. Those who are abused need to hand this unhealthy shame and guilt back to their abuser before they can more forward and heal. Unhealthy shame and guilt causes victims to feel unacceptable and hopelessly flawed. Shame falls away when survivors realize they are not to blame. When survivors hold the abuser accountable, the lies and secrets lose power over them.

If we turn to Jesus Christ and receive His love, we allow His influence to shine a light into all dark lies. Receiving the blessings of the Atonement helps us relearn how to love, expands our vision, deepens our joy, quickens our minds, strengthens our muscles, lifts our spirits, multiplies our blessings, increases our opportunities, comforts our souls, raises up friends, and pours out peace. If we allow Christ's love to work in us, we are able to experience healthy guilt, which allows us to see ourselves realistically and make positive changes when needed.

Every single person is an important and priceless son or daughter of God. We are all divinely loved and valued just the way we are today. No matter what others do to us or what mistakes we make, we never lose the love of God. Our eternal worth is constant and does not depend on what we or others do. Each of us has infinite worth and eternal potential.

THE DANGERS OF SELF-DECEPTION

When it comes to abuse, we deceive ourselves in the following ways:

- *Idealizing*—Refusing to admit that we or someone close to us has abused us.
- *Deceiving or denying*—Hiding the abuse.
- *Minimizing*—Taking no action because the abuse wasn't that bad.
- *Ignoring*—Telling ourselves we'll take care of it later.
- *Comparing*—Telling ourselves the abuse isn't as bad as that of someone else.
- *Justifying*—Believing we or others deserve to be abused.

If we refuse to face the truth and instead cling to the blindness of self-deception, we misunderstand the nature of accountability. Abuse is like a circle that never ends until someone in the circle is willing to give up his false reality. For instance, overcoming self-deception when we abuse others, are abused, or witness abuse includes giving up the lie that the person who was abused deserved it or that we or they are powerless to do anything about it. We can take steps to improve our acceptance of reality. The first step an offender must take is admitting that he or she is an abuser. The first step a victim takes is recognizing he or she is or was abused. The first step a bystander takes is admitting he or she failed to protect someone from abuse. If we ask for help, God will help us see the truth about our circumstances and give us the courage to repent or forgive and the divine power to heal.

Facing the truth may seem terrifying, but once done, we will find that fear and guilt no longer rule us. As long as we wait for someone else to change, we remain tangled in the web of abuse. It is a great act of love to no longer allow others to abuse us. Even Jesus Christ cannot save us if we believe we deserve to be abused. When we are so self-deceived that we believe abuse is our lot in life, we make the Atonement void in our lives.

Self-deception keeps us from feeling God's love. As we go to our Savior with a broken heart and a contrite spirit and receive the gifts of the Atonement, God will reveal to us how beloved we truly are and what infinite potential we already possess. When we emerge into the light of God's love, we can look at and discard all the lies we accepted as truth. All lies melt in the radiant reality of God's infinite love.

Knowing the truth about our worth allows us to step into divinely revealed knowledge about our potential. We no longer depend on what we've seen, heard, or experienced from other human beings to properly instruct us about the nature of who we really are. Only God can tell us who we are and what we need to do. As we move forward with faith that our Father in Heaven will provide all we need, we will feel God's love in a deeply personal and sacred way. God can do so much more with us than we can do with ourselves.

We can overcome our previous inability to protect ourselves from an abuser. "If men come unto me I will show unto them their weakness. I give unto men weakness that they may be humble; and my grace is sufficient for all men that humble themselves before me;

for if they humble themselves before me, and have faith in me, then will I make weak things become strong unto them" (Ether 12:27). As we receive the gifts of the Atonement, our will and God's will become one. Then we are endowed with "the love of God" (1 Nephi 11:22). When we personally feel the unconditional love of our Heavenly Father, we don't need anything else.

Chapter Four

ENDING AN ABUSIVE RELATIONSHIP

I t's never too late to end an abusive relationship. Once we truly comprehend all the consequences of destructive relationships, we will find the courage to stop the pain. For some, this decision comes when we realize our life or mental stability is in danger. For others, this moment arrives when we comprehend that innocent children are being harmed by our failure to act. When a victim takes a courageous stand against oppressive behavior, it is a pinnacle moment in which light and truth triumph over darkness and lies. When an abuse survivor gives her mind and heart to the Savior and joins forces with the powers of heaven, the ennobling gifts of the Atonement become real and the journey to healing begins.

One woman described her decision to end her lifelong tolerance for her parents' abuse this way:

> One night I stood at my living-room window during a winter storm and watched my parents drive away. I didn't know if they'd ever come back or speak to me again. Before my parents arrived at my home, I'd tucked my young children into bed following story time. I was sitting on the sofa alone when the doorbell rang. When I opened the door and saw my parents, I invited them both inside, and we sat in the living room to talk. When my husband was present, my parents' conversations were kept cordial and light. But when I found myself alone with them, the conversation always turned into a personal attack on me or a rehash or new flurry of accusations my parents had for each other. Then that look of darkness I so feared as a child flashed across my mother's face.

"You're a total failure," my mother said. "How much can you be worth if your own mother doesn't love you?"

I'd heard words like those hundreds of times before, both as a child and as an adult. Previously I told myself I had to take it because they were my parents. I'd always stuffed my pain so I didn't have to feel it, but that night I allowed myself to feel. Tight physical weight pressed down on my chest, making it difficult to breathe. The temperature in the room seemed to plummet; my pulse quickened, and I shook uncontrollably. I shifted my eyes to my father, waiting for him to respond in some way, any way. He sat silently next to my mother, refusing to make eye contact.

As I glanced at my father, I remembered watching Mom hurl a fork at him across the dinner table one night, catching him between the eyes. Blood trickled into his glass of water, turning it pink. When I was a child, I had nowhere to go to be safe and no one I could count on to protect me. As the years went by, I was also increasingly convinced I must be the problem. If I were a better person, my parents would stop hurting me. So I bent and twisted myself into every version of the person I thought they wanted so they would love me. Nothing worked. The whole family remained trapped by my parents' toxic marriage.

That night as I sat in the living room facing both my parents, I fully experienced what was happening to me.

This is the pain of knowing my parents don't love me.

That was the unspeakable truth I'd run from all my life. My whole body trembled like it belonged to someone else. Then I made a conscious choice to reconnect with my body and feel my own anguish.

This is fear.

Finally facing my darkest reality overwhelmed my sense of security with the terror of countless days and nights of repressed grief.

This is rejection.

I wanted to cease to be so I could relieve my pain. Yet I could not move or make a sound. I did not know grief felt so much like fear. I closed my eyes, fully expecting a wave of sorrow to drag me into a black abyss.

Dear God, please help me, I prayed.

At the very instant that I called on help beyond this world, it was as if a veil of darkness lifted. I realized with increasing mental clarity that I could survive this. I could stand in my greatest fear and not be overcome. Strength beyond my own literally joined forces with my mind, body, and spirit.

I can feel this pain and still live, I thought with a rising sense of surprise and relief.

That was the moment when I clearly understood for the first time what I needed to do. I realized I couldn't change my parents, but I could change me. I was beginning to understand their inability to love me was unrelated to me. At the same time, I also understood what they were doing to me was wrong and had to stop. I realized that if I said nothing or continued to ignore their behavior, fruitlessly hoping things would get better, I would continue to be a player in our sick and painful family legacy. I was an adult and capable of setting healthy boundaries in my own home. My husband was out of town. The younger children were asleep, and the older children were away. I was alone to face my Goliath.

Dear God, teach me how to love them.

When that desire flooded my being, it was as if I gained access to an illuminating and strengthening power beyond myself. Though I knew I loved my mother and father, I understood that if I responded to their present behavior as though it were acceptable, I would be withholding truth and continuing a legacy of tolerating abuse. Quite unexpectedly, I was open to the possibility that my parents were also in pain. I wondered—if I looked more closely, forgetting my rejection just for a moment—would I be able to see something I had been missing? I realized some event in their past or some other personal limitation apart from me contributed to their behavior. I mentally separated my need to face reality and protect myself and my need to judge them. At the same time I also knew I could no longer brush off cruel encounters hoping our relationship would get better someday. I knew our interactions would go smoothly for a while and then the abuse would happen again and again and again. I could no longer split reality, telling myself something that would make their damaging treatment all right.

"I love you, Mom and Dad," I said, shaking. "I need you to understand this is my home. I want people to feel safe here, including me. If we can have a healthy adult conversation here tonight, you're free to stay. If not, I'll have to ask you to leave."

Though I was hoping we could end the present abusive conversation and try again, I wasn't surprised when both my father and mother rose, silently slipped on their wool coats, and left in a huff. I parted the curtains and watched them both slowly drive away, leaving long, dark tire trails in the lightly fallen snow. That was the first time in my life I'd insisted on being treated with respect. It was both terrifying and liberating. The relationship I had with my parents changed that night. As I watched them leave, I knew how deeply I loved them. I'd spent a lifetime longing for their approval and affection, but I was no longer naïve, desperate, or needy. I no longer gave my quiet consent, forever hoping things would get better someday. I no longer grasped for their attention and love at the price of my peace of mind and self-respect. Today, I'm not burdened with my past, because I've chosen the journey of healing made possible by the Atonement of Jesus Christ. I don't have to judge anybody; God knows, and only He can make final judgments. Though my extended family remains entangled in destructive relationships, I've made a choice to leave abusive relationships behind and move forward with my life.

A TIME TO CHOOSE

Children lack the knowledge and skills to stop the abuse they experience. However, adults have a choice. We are not powerless. No one can continue to abuse us without our consent. We are not victims; we are targets with legs. We can move out of shooting range. No one has to stand still for target practice. If we are or have been in an abusive relationship, we are wounded. Before we can even begin to heal, we need to understand that safety is an absolute prerequisite. We can't heal from damage if we are allowing more damage to occur at the same time. We can't heal from a gunshot wound if we're standing in front of someone who is still shooting at us.

If we want to be at peace with God and ourselves, to feel joy and fulfill our potential in life, we need to face and deal with all our destructive relationships. Abuse is not compatible with any gospel principle and should not be tolerated. We do not deserve to be abused; being treated without respect is no one's lot in life. We are not being patient, loving, or forgiving if we allow abuse to continue; we are permitting our destruction and gravely harming the next generation.

Most like to think of their destructive relationship as the exception. Though research proves otherwise, many victims believe their abuser will change if they just love them enough or hang in there long enough. They deceive themselves with excuses for the abuser's cruel behavior and their decision to stay in the relationship. If we want to heal, we have to understand that we can't change or save our abuser—only Jesus Christ can. And if we are allowing someone to continue to abuse us, we may actually be preventing him from being saved. We can't begin the healing process until we face the truth and hold our abuser accountable.

One woman described the moment she faced her fears. It began with a predawn walk.

> One day on my morning walk, I reached a familiar intersection. If I walked straight ahead, I'd have to take the chance of meeting up with two unrestrained hunting dogs that had previously attacked me. If I turned left, I could avoid the situation. Sometimes the dogs would be running loose and other times they would be tied up. In the past I'd taken my chances, hoping for the best. But after one of the dogs bit me, I was forced to take action. I alerted the local animal control authorities and the owners were warned. For a while this strategy worked. But soon the dogs were running lose again. I decided to adjust my routine and change my route. This particular day when I got to the intersection of choice, I stopped and took a deep breath. Something inside me couldn't turn left. I was tired of being threatened. I'd had enough. So I continued walking. Sure enough, those dogs came again at full speed. My heart was pounding and I wanted to run—but I could not avoid this situation any longer. I was sick and tired of being the same old scared me. Right when those two huge dogs were about to attack, I abruptly threw my arms into the air and yelled, "You stupid dogs, leave me alone and get out of here!"
>
> To my total surprise, both animals stopped and quickly retreated. I kept walking straight ahead. This was an empowering moment for me because the courage I found to face those dogs soon became new courage to face my human attackers. Now I understand I have a choice every time an abuser comes at me. I can avoid the situation or I can refuse to be frightened or controlled. As a child I had no choice; I was trapped in an abusive situation. As an adult, I must face my deepest fears. I have learned to let go, not of love, but of those who do not love. I choose to face the beast, feel the loss, walk through the pain, and heal.

CONSEQUENCES OF ABUSE

Unhealed abuse often lies at the core of addiction, violence, mental health issues, unhealthy associations, and estrangements. Destructive relationships play a huge part in compulsive, illegal, or immoral behavior, along with materialism, competitiveness, jealousy, apostasy, and divorce. When we look for pain instead of blame, we are better able to remove ourselves from destructive relationships without bitterness. We understand that people who are hurt, hurt people. Even though it is not safe for us to have a relationship with someone who abuses us, we can forgive them and move forward with our lives. When we are motivated by love to stop abuse, we will be given opportunities to heal.

Some people who have been abused struggle with powerful feelings of love or hate for the abuser that bind them to a destructive relationship. It helps to remember that loving someone is fundamentally different from having a loving relationship with someone. Someone who is abusing us is not capable of having a loving relationship with us. We can also overcome the confused belief that tells us to stay in a destructive relationship because we think we have to in order to keep the commandments.

Hating an abuser also binds us to them because we allow the abuser to control our thoughts and behavior, effectively keeping ourselves from feeling joy and peace. Some abuse survivors transfer this hate to innocent people or God. Hate keeps us in the victim role and stops our character development. Recognizing, developing, and maintaining a loving relationship with yourself, God, and other healthy, nonabusive people is the goal. People who haven't healed from abuse don't know how to love, for they've never been loved. They can't rescue anyone because they're in desperate need of rescue themselves. They don't know how to cherish others because they've never been cherished. We need to understand that it is impossible for wounded mortals to free themselves from the tangled web of destructive relationships without God's help.

The nature of abuse makes it hard for victims and abusers to see beyond their warped relationships to the only true escape route— God's love and Christ's infinite Atonement. In our desperate search for happiness and peace, too many of us waste our lives fruitlessly waiting for wounded mortals to love us, effectively forgetting the Savior already has. No human love compares to God's infinite love. No mortal has done for us what Christ has done. Before we can feel divine love, we have to take the Savior's outstretched hand and let Him pull us from our destructive relationship.

FACING REALITY

When victims finally face the reality that their abuser is not going to change and it is not safe to have a relationship with that person, they often feel lost about what they are going to do with the rest of their lives. Many victims report that they have to go through a period of profound fear, anxiety, and mourning after their choice to leave. Yet they also report an increasing sense of relief, freedom, and strength. They become the change they seek in their lives. They are no longer held back or controlled. They stop rewarding their abuser for what he did by effectively giving him not only their past but their future as well. They become a transitional character in their family. They form new healthy relationships where they can love and be loved. They reprogram their minds with truth and move into a future where they can fulfill their potential.

Abuse survivors find it liberating to realize they don't have to pass final judgment on the abuser; they need only understand that some people are full of rage, enmity, aggression, or deviancy and they cannot be around them without getting hurt. Those who invite Christ into their healing don't waste their lives seeking revenge; they simply choose to keep themselves safe. They don't feel the need to punish anyone—including themselves—and finally and fully receive the grace of God.

All experience in mortality grants us the opportunity to gain new knowledge about the tension of opposition—good and evil, pleasure and pain, grief and joy, sickness and health, light and darkness, life and death. We are constantly pulled. When we see only one side of each experience, we don't obtain fulness. We increase our ability to become more like God when we experience the tension between good and evil and then, of our own free will, choose the good.

We all meet with disappointment and pain in our lives. What's important is what we do when faced with that pain. Some turn to addictive substances and behaviors, while others retreat into chronic physical or mental illness or suffer with depression, obsessive thoughts, or compulsive behavior. We can choose to learn more effective patterns of adjustment that move us forward into forgiveness and love. We can seek out ecclesiastical and professional help so we can develop the necessary tools to change our inner reality and outer circumstances. We can exchange our unhealthy patterns of adjustment for healthy ones. If we've been abused, we've suffered a deep wound to our soul that requires divine healing. Our previous way of thinking, behaving, and living needs to be dramatically redirected and reeducated; otherwise, the adverse effects of abuse will control our present and future lives as well.

LIFE IS HARD, AND THEN WE LIVE

In essence, life is hard—and then life goes on. Life is full of pain and joy. We can't have one without the other. Problems and challenges never go away, but they will change to new ones if we're moving forward with our own personal spiritual development. If we're dealing with the same old abuse issues, year after year, we need to change. We can't change the abuser. We have to quit running from our profound loneliness, grief, abandonment, betrayal, and rejection and instead face and feel them. All unhealed pain has a way of remaining deep in our subconscious no matter how fast we run. There is no real escape from fear or pain by avoidance. We must allow ourselves to feel the anguish—all of it. Feeling deep personal pain teaches us truths we learn no other way.

The following account is how one man described allowing himself to heal after feeling the deep personal pain caused by his alcoholic father:

> After I allowed myself to actually feel the pain of my father's rejection, I learned I could survive it. The next time I felt rejected by someone, I allowed myself to feel the pain because I knew I could survive it and become stronger with each attempt. I learned that by allowing myself to feel pain, I also opened my heart to feel joy, and I didn't have to face my pain alone. I took the Savior's hand and

looked at my painful past with him. He revealed to me all I had gained after all I've lost. I've learned that if we want to heal, there is no way around pain; we can only go through.

For me, the abuse cycle involved a lack of connection with my own feelings. I kept going back to my father, hoping for a good relationship but being abused again and again. When I honestly allowed myself to feel the pain of his cruel behavior, I could not put myself though that horrible ordeal again. I remember that life-changing day clearly. I let myself feel everything. I was spread eagle on the floor in my bedroom one afternoon when I was home alone. It was awful—groaning sounds coming from my mouth I'd never heard before. But the intensity of the pain passed. I never willingly placed myself in an abusive situation with my father again.

I learned that you can't get love from an abuser. You have to cut your losses and move on. I was able to move forward when I surrounded myself with healthy, loving people and activities that I enjoy. I choose to focus my time and energy on my wife and children, rather than constantly trying to fix relationships with family members who, quite frankly, never changed.

Healing from abuse can't be forced or hurried. Healing moves through stages and progresses from denial to awareness, from seeking justice to seeking mercy, and finally to receiving power from God to forgive, love, and move forward. There is no rigid timetable. Healing takes as long as it takes. The healing that follows an acceptance of the Atonement is not a forgetting of the abuse—it is a step-by-step releasing of the negative thoughts and behaviors we have developed because of abuse. If we truly want to move forward, we can no longer stand at the window of opportunity with our hearts closed, protected but blind to what is going on outside the narrow prison of our disappointment and pain. We have to look to the higher power of God's love and then choose the ennobling freedom of repentance and forgiveness.

Living through the difficulties of life gives us the best opportunity in mortality to practice every sanctifying gospel principle. Without the constant complexities of relationships, we would never see inside or outside ourselves sufficiently or feel our personal need for the Atonement of Jesus Christ. As we choose to repent and forgive even after knowing great heartache, God's love will clean our soul and let in the light. After we go through the process of receiving the Atonement, our Creator will endow us with the ability to love. Though there is much we don't understand in mortality, through the grace of God, we can trust that everything we experience will work toward our good. Everything we don't understand today will be understood someday. We can trust God completely. True peace is a gift from God following obedience to commandments, not a result of how others treat us.

We will constantly be confronted with challenges and problems in this life, but if we give ourselves to God with a broken heart and contrite spirit, our souls will find peace and we will experience joy. Our problems won't disappear, but our capacities to endure will enlarge, our wisdom will increase, our patience will expand, and we will live our lives with deeper purpose and meaning. We will be sanctified, or made holy, by our trials. If we allow Christ's Atonement to heal us, we can literally call down blessings from heaven upon our household.

Windows in our soul have two sides: one that allows us to look inside, and one, outside. When we access the Atonement, we keep the glass sufficiently clean so that our view is not obstructed on either side. We need to look inside to repent and purify ourselves, and we need to look outside to learn how to forgive and love.

If we keep our covenants, opportunities to heal are always open to us. Because our Savior will ultimately cleanse and heal us from sin, we don't have to grit our teeth and endure. We abide in our challenges with a joyful heart and endure well. Too many of us live in darkness. We can let go of our pain and fear and give our hearts to God. "Fear not: for I have redeemed thee," the Savior said. "I have called thee by thy name; thou art mine. When thou passest through the waters, I will be with thee" (Isaiah 43:1–2).

We can't fix others, but we can repent of our own sins, forgive, and learn how to love. As we are healing, God will lead us to others who are in pain. Because of what we have gone through, we will know better how to succor those with great sorrow. We will no longer be ruled by fear or shame. We will arise from our pain with a new compassion born of personal experience, a new depth of hope born of our own rebirth into joy.

Section Two

HOW TO STOP ABUSE

Chapter Five

LOOKING INSIDE

T he best way to stop abuse is to start with ourselves. Good and evil are the results of personal choices. No matter what has happened to us, God grants us the opportunity to choose a better way. The Atonement makes it possible for us to see ourselves as a beloved child of God with the power to choose light over darkness. No matter what we have experienced in our past, we can choose a better tomorrow.

The following account is how one woman described her experience at a pivotal moment that literally changed her life and stopped her from handing down the abusive legacy she had been given:

> I remember with razor precision the day when something happened between my daughter and me that changed my life. When my daughter was a small child, she made a mistake that infuriated me. My heart raced in anger, believing she needed to be punished. Making a split-second choice, I slapped her. Immediately after that slap, I looked into her eyes and saw something that took my breath away. I had a momentary glimpse inside her heart, the part I had just broken. Before my choice to slap her, she knew she could trust me. My angry slap had broken her confidence and violated her childlike trust in my goodness—and her own. Yet even worse, I saw something more—the look that told me she believed my lie, believed she was a bad girl and deserved to be treated disrespectfully. I understood that I was lying to her so she would believe my sin was hers. She believed she was a bad girl and deserved to be hurt. At that moment, everything in the room blurred—except for her eyes welling up with tears.

An immense heaviness hit me. I was overcome with the understanding that I was the adult and it was my responsibility to control myself. My daughter was my divine stewardship, and I was deeply aware I was never to abuse my power as her mother to hurt her. As my little daughter looked at me with deep sadness, I felt the consequences of what I'd done. I felt a penetrating mourning so deep that I fell to my knees.

"I'm so sorry I hit you. I'm your mama. I'm supposed to protect you and love you."

"No, Mama, you should hit me," she answered. "I'm a bad girl."

"No, you're not a bad girl," I answered. "You made a mistake. You're not a bad girl. You're wonderful. I love you. Will you please forgive me?"

She thought for a minute before she smiled, then responded, "You're not a bad mommy. You made a mistake. I love you too." Then she wrapped her soft, pudgy arms around my neck and gently patted the top of my head to comfort me.

As I knelt there in my daughter's embrace, all my years growing up as a child roared back into my head like a lightning flash during a thunderstorm. Playing before my eyes as if it were on a huge movie screen, I saw my raging mother standing over me with a roller-skate, smashing the metal wheels into my face over and over again. I saw her black eyes and heard her screams: "You ugly, fat, disgusting piece of vomit. I hate your guts. I wish you'd never been born."

While my daughter and I held each other, I realized for the first time that I had not deserved to be hurt when I was a child. I was not a bad little girl. I understood all children are innocent, vulnerable, and precious. After that moment with my daughter, my mother's insistence that I had deserved her cruel treatment no longer held me hostage. Her oft-used excuses were exposed as lies. As I held my tiny daughter in my arms, I understood on a deep and profound level that no child deserves to be hurt.

"I love you," I whispered to my tiny daughter.

As I spoke those words in our mutual embrace, I felt my daughter's forgiveness and love like healing warmth moving from the top of my head, through my body, and out the ends of my toes. A gentle wholeness lifted me, expanding my mind with an increased understanding of what was true and false, what was good and evil. I knew I was capable of both; the decision was mine. I knew, beyond any doubt, that I could never hurt my child again or anyone else without realizing the pain I was causing and the lie I was telling. The worth of my daughter's soul was made known to me in such a way that I understood the power and trust that had been given to me as her mother. At the same instant, I understood that same power and trust had been given to my mother. She had made a choice.

After that experience with my daughter, I knew on a penetrating level I had numerous changes to make in myself so I could truly love her. My desire to control her, even for her own good, could not abide in me anymore. That desire was replaced with a yearning to know my daughter, to learn how to love her and teach her the truth about God, the world, and herself. Since I didn't know how, I had to ask my Heavenly Father for help.

It takes painful introspection to examine our capacity to harm or heal. The only way to stop abuse in this world is for each of us to refuse to be a perpetrator, bystander, or victim. The only way to reach that important decision is to recognize abuse and take responsibility to stop cruel behavior—both the pain we cause and the pain someone else is causing.

Understanding Evil

The capacity for evil resides in all of us. Each of us has to face it, own it, and then with our free will choose a better way. Though we seldom contemplate the gravity of our personal choices, the actions we take every day affect the eternities. We cannot do good or evil without the rippling effects of our actions circling out and touching other lives. A flawed illusion of separateness, or the belief that what we do impacts only ourselves, is often the beginning point of suffering for others. We need to look inside our hearts and homes first and examine our own motives and actions with great personal honesty. We make little progress in discerning between good and evil by only pointing fingers at all the sinners out there. We need to constantly examine ourselves first to obtain a clear view of the sinner inside.

Evil is most often manifest by the abuse of power. Those with power over others have the responsibility to use that power to bless, not harm; build, not tear down; and inspire, not control. Evil is also a personal state of mental darkness or self-inspection blindness coupled with a refusal to acknowledge personal sin and submit to God's laws. And, unfortunately, efforts to escape guilt often result in more evil. Evil is accompanied by pride, self-absorption, selfishness, lack of humility, and self-deception, along with arrogance and a refusal to submit to any will other than our own. Many of us believe that the most evil people among us reside in jail when, in fact, many live hidden in our own families and communities. Many escape suffering in this life because they never admit to or feel the pain they've caused and never correct wrongdoing. But the people around them suffer. Those who abuse leave their carnage in broken human hearts strewn in a long path of family and societal destruction. How we treat our family members and associates may have the greatest impact for good or ill of anything we'll ever do in our lives. Those who abuse or do nothing to stop abuse turn off the light of God's love.

It is important to understand that evil is not always obvious, even though it is both common and ordinary. Evil is the will that resides inside each of us that seeks to dominate or control others, to tear down, discourage growth, diminish originality, and cause despair. Evil is opposition to life. In fact, the very word *evil* is *live* spelled backward. Evil is the wounding of body or spirit. Evil is a false sense of entitlement or superiority.

Evil deceives, injures, diminishes, punishes, wounds, labels, damages, attacks, corrupts, condemns, denigrates, and denies. It manipulates, controls, humiliates, belittles, vilifies, ignores, threatens, tortures, frightens, and neglects. In essence, evil kills life, hope, awareness, warmth, and light. Those who choose evil are dishonest with themselves, for evil is unreality. They see others as oppressors and lose the ability to see themselves as they really are. They refuse to feel how their cruel actions cause anguish for those around them.

Abusers seek control; in order to keep control, they often seek to eliminate unpredictability, liveliness, spontaneity, and goodness. They desperately need to avoid guilt and self-examination, for evil resides not entirely in the sin but in the refusal to acknowledge sin. Abusers refuse to see their own need to repent, to suffer the pain of self-purification, and to feel the anguish they have caused. They refuse to see the truth about themselves and seldom if ever admit that their actions are wrong. Without the courage to face the truth and change, both abusers and victims never break free of the abuse cycle. Instead they surround themselves with lies, insulating their souls against pain. Only through accepting the truth, no matter how painful, can we access the power of the Atonement.

PERSONAL HONESTY BRINGS PERSONAL GROWTH

Personal honesty means we look at ourselves first to see if we are harming those around us. When we are willing to change our thoughts, words, and actions, we allow the power of heaven to assist us. We do not have to live in a state of anxiety, fear, and hopelessness. "For God hath not given us the spirit of fear; but of power, and of love, and of a sound mind" (2 Timothy 1:7). If we feel afraid and powerless, God is not the source of those feelings. As daughters and sons of Deity, we have great untapped power we can access through daily purification. When we call on divine assistance through sincere prayer, all things are possible, even changing our very hearts. As we seek to become the change we seek in the world, our image of God as an angry judge—assigning penalties for our sins—will change forever. We will discover God will always lovingly provide us with the assistance we require to reach our potential.

The need for repentance and forgiveness comes from deep inside us. Even if God could forgive us without our repentance, we wouldn't be able to accept it, for each of us has an innate understanding about the need for a balance between justice and mercy. As we are in the process of changing ourselves, we will find that God is not someone to fear, but to love. Repentance is not something to resist, but to crave. As we strive daily to repent and forgive, God will enlarge our capacity to love and be loved. With love, all things are possible.

Satan's power depends on our willingness to believe his lies. Some of those lies involve self-deception or discouragement. In other words, we either don't see our need to change or we are too overwhelmed to even try. Godly sorrow, on the other hand, allows us to see our own wrongdoing and at the same time gives us the strength to make personal improvements.

Our choice to love and bless or abuse and control others will be repeated in the lives of all those we influenced in mortality. Perhaps it will be "hell" to watch how our bad choices ripple out and negatively impact innumerable lives. Perhaps it will be "heaven" to watch how our loving actions ripple out and positively impact innumerable lives. Daily we choose what kind of existence we will experience after death.

This life is an opportunity to learn new and deeper levels of submission to God's will, by degrees, through personal choice. Most of us want only one opinion about ourselves: our own. Daily, prayerful self-examination is needed, for all our sins are reparable—though we're much impeded by the sin of believing we are without sin. We need to live in such a way that we can feel God's love for us every day and at the same time develop a continuing recognition of our constant need for the Atonement of Jesus Christ. Then we can help others feel God's love for them by the way we treat them. True discipleship is manifest by the way we treat each other.

Journalists are taught that stories with only one source are often inaccurate and unbalanced. They are instructed to research and explore the various sides to every issue and are advised to obtain opposing viewpoints for their article topics so readers will have a more balanced and accurate perspective. In a similar manner, we should purposely seek out—through sincere prayer—views contrasting with our own about individual and family concerns. When we constantly seek to be self-enlightened, we will often be surprised by our own deeply guarded self-deception.

CHOOSING NOT TO MAKE ANY MORE INNOCENTS SUFFER

We can't repent for the abuser. We can't atone for someone else's sins—only the Savior can. Yet we can recognize that we may be continuing the abuse we suffered by abusing ourselves or causing another innocent person to suffer. If we want to untangle ourselves from the web of destructive relationships, we must take personal responsibility in the present for allowing any innocent person to suffer, including ourselves.

For example, one woman told me her father abused her when she was a child. She subsequently feared men and spent the majority of her life overeating in a subconscious effort to keep men away from her. She believed the lies she heard about her appearance and potential as a child and continued abusing herself with negative, self-loathing thoughts and poor health habits. When she finally realized she was allowing her father's abuse to continue through her own actions, she didn't know how to stop. She sought God's help. These are the questions she asked in prayer: "Father in Heaven, do you love me? Please, teach me who I am. What are my gifts?" This woman told me that finding the answers to those questions was the first step on her journey to healing.

Personal introspection allows us to be scrupulously honest and make the conscious choice to stop the suffering. From this choice can come healing for generations past, present, and future. For instance, one woman told me her grandfather sexually abused her as a young child. Her grandfather died when she was a teenager and before she told anyone about the abuse.

After she married, this woman told her mother. Her mother admitted that the same person, her father, had sexually abused her as a child as well. She told the daughter she thought the abuse ended with her, and she wished the daughter had never mentioned the abuse because it only added to her pain. Then she asked the daughter not to tell anyone else because she didn't want her father remembered that way. This mother never took responsibility for allowing her daughter to be alone with a person she knew to be a child sexual abuser. Because the mother was an unhealed victim, she was emotionally unavailable and responded to her daughter's cries for help inappropriately, compounding the guilt and shame of both of them.

This woman told me she finally realized her mother could not be the person to help her because she was not willing to help herself. The daughter sought professional counseling and spiritual guidance from her bishop. At some point in her long and difficult healing process, this woman said, she realized she'd been forcing her husband to pay the price for her abuse. When her husband approached her for intimacy, she rebuffed him. She realized her husband had spent many lonely years feeling rejected and unloved because of her. She was forcing her innocent husband to suffer for her past abuse. When she realized what she was doing, she asked for his forgiveness, and together they sought counseling to heal their marriage.

This woman said that in the process of healing, she was finally able to fully accept that she was not guilty of and did not need to repent for the abuse she suffered as a child by her grandfather, even if she did nothing to stop it. She learned that little children don't consent; they obey. She was not guilty of adding to her mother's pain by telling her of the abuse. She had courageously given her mother a new opportunity to heal from her own past.

Though her mother never took full accountability for her lack of protection and her emotional unavailability, the daughter told me she was no longer held back by her mother's choices. With her new softened heart, she and her husband were able to work on her intimacy issues together. This woman also took it upon herself to educate the children in her community about the reality of abuse and how to protect themselves.

When we willingly acknowledge that we've done something wrong—either by abusing ourselves or others or by tolerating or hiding abuse—we allow God's love to enter our lives. As we seek first to improve ourselves, we will be reborn and given the exalting power to change and heal through the Atonement of Jesus Christ.

Chapter Six

PREVENTING ABUSE

I f we want to prevent abuse, we must start with children and
the adults who care for them. We all need specific information
about unacceptable ways for human beings to treat each other.
Contrary to what many adults believe, it is never acceptable to
harm children. Children also need to know that not all adults
should be obeyed. Children have controlling messages drilled into
their heads: You must obey me because I'm your father, mother,
or teacher. They're often punished in harsh ways when they don't
comply. Abusers know children have been preconditioned to obey
and will take advantage of their innocence and vulnerability.

INSTRUCTION ON ABUSE PREVENTION

Each of us needs to make sure that instruction on abuse prevention is being taught in our family, church group, school, and
community. All abuse-prevention instruction should include this
vital message: No one has the right to hurt you or make you feel
bad or scared inside. Church leaders, school teachers, and parents
should teach children to say no whenever they feel uncomfortable,
scared, or worried about what that is happening to them. Instruction should include practicing possible scenarios where children
might be abused and teaching children how to respond to, avoid, or
report the situation. Children also need to be taught to tell a trusted
adult outside the family if a family member hurts them or touches
the private parts of their body.

Adults shouldn't look the other way when children hurt each other at home, on the playground, or at church. Parents should know that current Church policy mandates that all Primary classes and youth activities are to be taught or supervised by a woman alone, a man and a woman, or two men. We can all insist that our children's teachers at school have in-class aides, doctors have exam-room assistants, and playgrounds be supervised by at least two adults. Parents have the right to carefully screen friends and restrict sleepover parties.

When children have the courage to tell adults about abuse, they should not be labeled as exaggerators, fabricators, or tattletales, but should be rewarded with prompt attention and swift consequences for perpetrators. When we assume children are mistaken or look the other way, we are part of the problem.

One woman described her difficult attempts to stop the abuse in her life this way:

> I remember my teacher at church giving me a lesson about obeying your parents. I would hear this lesson over and over. I felt my heart pounding in my chest. I wanted to ask her a question, but I was afraid.
>
> Finally I mustered the courage to ask, "What if they hurt you?"
>
> "Your parents would never hurt you," she answered "Your daddy's in the bishopric. Maybe you do bad things, and they have to punish you. But they only punish you because they love you. God said we have to honor our parents. It's one of the Ten Commandments."

Those who don't understand the gravity of abuse and those who have never experienced it unknowingly reinforce the dark lies abused children learn at home. One lie is this: You are bad and deserve to be punished. Consequently, one of the best ways to prevent abusive behavior is to better educate children—and the adults who care for them—that children are not bad and do not deserve to be punished. Children are precious and innocent and deserve to be taught and corrected with gentleness and love.

Family abuse is a learned behavior transmitted from one generation to another and generally continues until someone outside the family intervenes. Children who see or experience abuse are more likely to become future perpetrators or permanent victims. Our laws already recognize this problem by making it a crime to commit abuse in the presence of children. Everyone deserves a safe environment. All parents need to set rules, such as no shouting, name-calling, hitting, threatening, rudeness, or put-downs; then they should model the behavior they want their children to copy. Parents need to set acceptable behavior rules for the home and teach their children how to repent and forgive by their example in the home.

All communities need education and empowerment courses that send these messages:

- Because you are special, no one has the right to hurt you.
- You don't have the right to hurt someone unless they're hurting you; then you have the right to stop them.
- When someone hurts you, it's not your fault.
- If anyone tries to trick you or make you feel bad inside, it's not your fault. For example, some people pretend to be your friend and then do something that hurts you or makes you feel bad inside.
- When someone is hurting you, you should tell a trusted adult what is happening.
- You have the right to hit or yell at anyone who is hurting you until they stop.
- When someone hurts or scares you, run and tell someone immediately.
- If you are in danger, run and tell a trusted adult what is happening.
- You have the right to defend yourself from anyone who is hurting you.
- You have the right to insist your school has a uniform defensive action to let others know you are being hurt—such as holding up your hands and yelling "STOP!" so adults on duty will know you need help.

SEX EDUCATION

Children should be taught the facts of human sexuality on an age-appropriate level, including the reason we are created male and female and have bodies that respond in certain ways to fulfill God's plan of happiness. Children need to know they always have the right to say no to another person's advances to touch them. Children should be taught that no one—stranger, acquaintance, or family member—has the right to touch, either over or under their clothing, the private parts of their body that are covered with a swimming suit. If children tell a parent about an abuse experience and the parent fails to act, the child should go to another trusted adult outside the family. Parents have the first and primary responsibility to teach sex education to their children plainly and honestly in the home. To help parents teach this sensitive and important information to their children, the Church has published *A Parent's Guide*. Children should be taught to love and take good care of their bodies. We need to teach the real names, as opposed to the nicknames, for all body parts. Children need to learn from their parents about intimate relationships between men and women and what standards of behavior God has set. Children need parents who are not embarrassed to discuss maturation, procreation, and God's law of chastity.

Parents need to be open, supportive, and loving when they teach their children about physical intimacy. They should teach children not to be ashamed of their feelings of attraction toward the opposite sex, but to be grateful for those feelings and the fulfillment they will experience after marriage. Adolescents need love and support as they deal with their confusing body changes and their curiosity about sexuality. Children need accurate information and loving parents with healthy attitudes about sexuality. Parents also have the responsibility to ensure that sex-education instruction given in school is consistent with their moral and ethical values. If the information given in school is not consistent with parental values, the parent has the responsibility to remove his child from the instruction.

DEALING WITH FAMILY MEMBER ABUSE

Adults need to deal with abuse issues within the family in a timely manner. Abuse problems do not disappear and generally grow larger over time. For example, one woman told me her brother-in-law sexually abused her when she was a child. She didn't have a name for what he did. When she told her mother, she shamed her into silence.

"Don't tell anybody about this or you'll ruin your sister's life," the mother said. So she didn't tell. This brother-in-law went on to molest many other young girls, including his own daughters. It was not the child's responsibility to do something about the abuse; it was her mother's as soon as she learned what happened.

It is against both moral and civil law not to report abuse when you know someone has been harmed. We can be held morally and legally responsible for failure to report. All forms of abuse leave wounds that need to heal. Emotional, mental, physical, or spiritual abuse should not be considered less severe than sexual abuse.

Victims often have mixed emotions when they seek accountability from their abuser. When an abuser is a parent, spouse, child, sibling, grandparent, or other close relative, emotional attachments have been formed that are difficult to sever without confusing and uncomfortable feelings of guilt, fear, relief, and uncertainty. Other family members are often unsupportive. Victims need the assistance of someone outside the family to help them through the process of holding the abuser accountable for her actions. Abusers often loom larger than life in the minds of victims. Abusers, in fact, are bullies who cower in the light of truth and courage. We can't let abusers spoil our lives because we are afraid of what they might do. No one should maintain a close relationship with someone who demeans and diminishes them after attempts to correct the situation. Facing the truth means we learn to expect and insist on nonabusive relationships.

Many individuals shy away from questions about the way they are or were treated. Yet as we gain a new awareness about what constitutes abuse and all the devastating results of cruel behavior, we can develop a specific plan to stop pain in its tracks before it does us or anyone else more harm. This plan should include a new insistence: I will treat others with respect, and I require others to treat me with respect. When we determine to put an end to abuse in all our relationships, it may appear to those who don't understand that we are breaking up the family. It is important to remember that abuse breaks up families—not the person who holds an abuser accountable and leaves the relationship for their own safety.

After a victim gives an abuser notice that cruel behavior will no longer be tolerated, he or she must be prepared for major life changes to occur. Added safety precautions, temporary or permanent separations, divorce, jail time, and excommunications may be necessary and can actually be the beginning of healing for a family where abusive behavior is a long-term, multigenerational pattern. Fortunately there is a growing awareness of and greater resistance to any type of abuse today.

By educating potential victims, helping present victims heal, and requiring perpetrators to face the consequences of their behavior, we can stop abuse before it moves to the next generation. Every parent, neighbor, teacher or school volunteer who teaches children and adults to protect themselves and report abuse; every man, woman, and child who tells their abuse story, however painful; every Church leader who reports abuse; every law enforcement officer who arrests a perpetrator; every judge and jury member who enforces the laws and demands a penalty is a hero and fulfills Christ's prediction for the last days: "The rebellious shall be pierced with much sorrow; for their iniquities shall be spoken upon the housetops, and their secret acts shall be revealed" (D&C 1:3).

THE CHURCH AND ABUSE

A critical responsibility of Church leaders and teachers is to teach members about abuse. Church leaders also help those who have been abused and protect those who may be vulnerable to future abuse. The Church has several printed resources to help members. They include *Responding to Abuse: Help for Ecclesiastical Leaders* and *Preventing and Responding to Spouse Abuse*. Members who want help understanding or removing themselves from an abusive situation can turn to their bishop or stake president. These leaders can consult with LDS Family Services, which has legal experts and specialists who can answer questions and formulate steps to keep victims safe. Church leaders can also arrange for abuse counseling. Charges can be adjusted based on the victim's ability to pay. Members also can contact LDS Family Services for help or to identify therapists whose approach is in harmony with gospel principles.

All members should report abuse to Church officials. Abuse should never be tolerated and the reporting of abuse should never be postponed, assuming the abuser will not abuse again. Studies have shown that abusers rarely stop until they receive the full legal and moral consequences. Reporting abuse and allowing Church officials to assist abusers through repentance and the legal process is the right thing to do. Properly viewed, Church discipline and legal consequences are not instruments of punishment, but vehicles for change.

CHURCH DISCIPLINE

Church discipline of offenders is up to the local bishop or stake president. After reporting abuse accurately and honestly, victims can leave matters in the hands of their local leaders. Victims can ruin their lives if they become bitter about a priesthood leader's decisions. Even if the abuser never confesses in this life or is never held accountable in ways the victim deems appropriate, the abuser's debt will eventually have to be paid. God knows the truth. "The Family: A Proclamation to the World" makes ultimate responsibility clear: "We warn that individuals who violate covenants of chastity, who abuse spouse or offspring, or who fail to fulfill family responsibilities will one day stand accountable before God."[1]

We can help both the abused and the abuser when we do the following:

- Educate ourselves about abuse.
- Respond quickly to acts or reports of abuse.
- Learn about and use services available for abuse victims in the area.
- Realize abuse can take place in any home.
- Require abusers to take responsibility for their actions.
- Plan or support meetings, firesides, and school programs on abuse.
- Never diminish the effects of abuse.
- Regard incidents of abuse as credible—false reports do occur but are rare.
- Never offer simplistic remedies.
- Realize forgiveness may be a slow process.
- Know that victims are not to blame—the abuser is responsible—always!

- Insist on a safe environment (if necessary, the offender must leave).
- Carefully study the scriptures and other good books about the Atonement.

The family and community are damaged when abuse happens and the adults choose to keep it secret. When no one helps the victim or holds the abuser accountable, we all eventually pay the price. Hurt people hurt many more people, including themselves.

Bringing to light the reason for the victim's pain is the first courageous step to uncovering a festering wound and administering the healing balm. Exposing abuse is not violating a trust. When a person leaves this life, his ability to repair the damage he or she has caused is hindered or negated. The time to stop abuse in every home and community is now.

NOTE

1. The Church of Jesus Christ of Latter-day Saints, "The Family: A Proclamation to the World," *Ensign*, Nov. 1995, 102.

Chapter Seven

HELP IS AVAILABLE FOR
ABUSE SURVIVORS

Studies show that abusers seldom change, so abuse will not stop unless victims change. Ending an abusive relationship sends this message: You are capable of better behavior, and I deserve better treatment. When someone refuses to take responsibility for their dangerous and destructive behavior, has no sense of guilt or sorrow for the havoc they cause, and takes no steps to improve, we must act in our own self-defense. When we remain in the relationship because of misplaced guilt or a misguided belief that things will get better if we just hold on, we find that our lives are trapped in the web of the abuser's cruel behavior.

These are the alternatives abuse survivors must choose between:

Remain in the relationship without changes and continue to be abused. Victims should realize if they do nothing, this is the choice they are making. Adults who remain in destructive relationships share the responsibility for the multitude of problems they and others develop from living with an abuser.

Continue the relationship but stop the abuse. This choice requires that we set new boundaries in the relationship. We must seek help outside the relationship, and abusers must be made accountable before this is a wise choice. Temporary or permanent separations give victims the time and safety required to determine if the abuser is capable of permanent change. All destructive and dangerous relationships have to dramatically change or end.

End the relationship. Ending a destructive relationship is frightening and life-changing—but sometimes it is necessary. Refusing to have contact with an unrepentant, abusive person is the right thing to do.

One woman described her gradual awakening to the abusive people in her life this way:

> Once I sat in a large ballroom during an awards ceremony at my university. I'd just received the outstanding student award from my department and the master of ceremonies was about to read the name of the winner for the entire college. When I heard my name called again, I thought they'd made a mistake. I sat there, stuck to my chair, hoping to give the master of ceremonies an opportunity to notice and call another student's name. These people obviously saw something in me I didn't recognize in myself.
>
> My husband had to nudge me to get me off the chair. When I returned to my seat, he smiled, hugged me, and said, "Way to go, honey."
>
> Then my mother leaned over and whispered into my ear, "I'll bet you think you're pretty hot stuff. Well, don't get a big head, because nothing you'll ever do will ever impress me."
>
> At the time I didn't know what my mother said was abusive. I'm not even sure I knew what verbal or emotional abuse was at that point in my life. All I knew was this: at every important or happy day of my life, some member of my extended family would ruin it by not showing up, causing a humiliating scene, or saying something demeaning or hateful. I never got used to it. It always hurt, but I had accepted it as the reality of my life.
>
> Gradually I learned what I was experiencing was called abuse. I'd always dealt with the cruel behavior of family members by believing a positive mental attitude could get me through anything. I now understand abuse is not something I need to get through, accept, or will away with positive thoughts. Abuse doesn't just go away; it has to be stopped. I had to remove myself from the destructive relationship. I had to stop tolerating abuse.

CREATING AN EXIT PLAN

In some cases, abusers are even more dangerous or vindictive when a victim decides to leave a destructive relationship. For that reason, each survivor who decides to end an abusive relationship should seriously consider asking for help from those who are trained professionally (police and social workers) and then proceed with a carefully thought-out plan with assistance by those who are trained. Victims need to know they can use the arm of the law to protect both themselves and other family members from further abuse. Here are some important items to consider:

Tell someone: Telling others about the abuse we are experiencing is not always a quick and simple solution, because others may lack important information. We must keep telling until we find someone who is helpful. We must be proactive to find the information and resources we need. Adults are responsible to establish a safe place to live for themselves and their children.

One woman described her difficulty in finding help this way:

> When I asked my father to make my mother stop hitting me, he told me to stop doing things to make her mad. When I told a policeman about abuse from my husband, he informed me that current laws made it impossible for him to arrest or place someone in a mental institution unless they are an imminent danger to themselves or others. When I told a victim's advocate about the abuse I was experiencing, she told me if she were me she'd change her name, move out of state, and never look back. For a long time, no one was helpful. I finally found a deputy that personally guided me through the process of obtaining a court order."

Documentation: Victims of abuse and those who want to help them should be advised that it is very important to document (phone recordings, journal entries, pictures, and so on) all threatening and abusive episodes or communications. The victim or a friend can keep a record of abuse and threats that includes dates and details. When we have a record, we don't have to rely on memory when we need this information later.

Emergency exit: All victims need an emergency exit plan and should collect the following in a safe and secret place: phone number for police, the domestic abuse hotline number, duplicate set of car keys, emergency money, copies of important documents, alternate secret living arrangements, packed suitcase, checkbook, bank records, credit cards, account numbers, social security numbers for self and children, medication, and so on.

Reporting: Any cruel or threatening behavior or any sexual mistreatment of ourselves or other family members should be reported to religious and legal authorities. Abuse is against the laws of the land and the laws of God. Law enforcement agencies (police), the courts, social service agencies, and corrections and probation officers are all waiting to serve abuse victims. If we have reason to believe someone outside our family is at risk, we also have the responsibility to report it. Suspicion and information can be anonymous.

Know your rights: Victims should know they can file a domestic violence complaint and ask for the abuser to be removed from the home. They can demand no further contact with the abuser, including phone or email. They can request custody of the children, temporary support, possession of the residence, and professional counseling.

Get the help of professionals: It is vital to end all abusive relationships with professional help. Crisis centers can secretly house an abused spouse and his or her children while victims are seeking protection through the legal system and a safe and secret place to live. It's important to be informed about the social services and law enforcement agencies locally available. When victims report abuse, they should take steps to ensure that they and any children involved will be safe from the abuser after they report. Social service agencies can provide safe and secret places for victims to stay, if necessary. Anyone who is concerned about their own, their child's, or another's welfare can anonymously call a hotline (listed below) to learn about the process of reporting abuse and how to protect themselves or others from the abuser after they report.

USING PROFESSIONAL HELP

Many victims are reluctant to call police, religious officials, or a social services agency because they are embarrassed and don't want people to know, they worry the abuser will retaliate, or they are concerned they won't be able to prove the abuse. If you are confused about the legal definition of abuse or lack information about how to gather evidence and make a report, you can contact your local law enforcement agency for help and guidance. Abuse hotlines are a useful way for victims to seek information anonymously.

Domestic abuse hotlines. Individuals can call the National Domestic Violence Hotline at 1-800-799-7233 to find the domestic-violence agency nearest to them. This service is available 24 hours a day, 365 days a year in the United States. Individuals can also contact the National Domestic Violence website at www.ndvh .org. Each state also has its own domestic violence hotline. Another resource is the Childhelp USA National Child Abuse Hotline. The toll-free number is 1-800-422-4453. This is completely confidential, and someone there will direct you to the Child Protective Services in your state. Childhelp USA is a nonprofit organization that has worked for many years for the safety of children through the treatment and prevention of child abuse. Their website is www .childhelpusa.org. Another helpful hotline is the Rape, Abuse, and Incest National Network at 1-800-656-4673. Callers will be guided to specialized services. Most countries have their own services for helping abuse victims. Victims can check the Internet for abuse hotlines, information, or services available in their area. Because computer use can be tracked, victims should use a computer at a safe location.

Local agencies and services for victims. If you've been abused or threatened, or know someone who has, you should contact your local law enforcement or social service agency for families. These services have various names such as Children's Advocacy Center or Center for Women and Children in Crisis. Each area has different abuse laws, so victims need to learn how to navigate the legal process. Social services are designed to educate, support, and walk victims through the legal system and keep them safe while they go through the process of obtaining court orders to protect themselves and other victims from further cruelty. The agency knows the laws in your state and can provide counseling and support. They've been there and understand. They believe you, guard your privacy, and surround you with powerful friends. They know how to make the system work for you. They are experts, and have multiple resources.

Court orders. Many victims fear that reporting abuse will not result in any real protection by local law enforcement agencies because abuse is often difficult to prove. This is where "no contact" orders and injunctions can be helpful. No-contact orders or injunctions are called a variety of names, including protective and restraining orders and stalking injunctions. Generally speaking, restraining orders are issued by a judge through the assistance of an attorney and protective orders are issued by a judge without the assistance of an attorney. Stalking injunctions are issued by a judge when abusers are not living with the victim. These orders demand that the abuser stay away from the victim (and sometimes other family members). While these court orders are not always effective, they are practical because they establish a record of abuse and put the offender on notice that a violation will be punished. That is always a good message to send. There is no cost for these court orders unless you involve the services of an attorney. Victims can also ask the court for ways to involve the services of an attorney without cost. Forms for no-contact orders and injunctions can be obtained through the local law enforcement agency where you live or the county or district attorney office in the nearest courthouse.

If a person violates a court order, they are in contempt of court and can be prosecuted. The violation will be placed on their criminal record. Most law enforcement and social service agencies have a person who is known as a victim's advocate who can walk abuse victims through the process and paperwork for obtaining protection through the legal system and establishing accountability for the abuser. The process of obtaining a court order for a victim's protection is simple but can seem foreign and intimidating. Victims are given an information sheet to fill out about themselves and the abuser. The victim will be asked to write a statement that details what abuse he or she is experiencing or has experienced, using— as much as possible—dates, times, and types of abuse, threats, or harassment. This is why documentation is helpful. A police official can help in this process by obtaining any past criminal records of the abuser, talking with witnesses, and advising victims on what other evidence they can gather.

After victims complete the forms, they will take their request for relief to their local courthouse. Most courthouses have a security system to keep you safe, much like the airports use. The victim will present his or her paperwork to a court clerk and will be asked to sign the written statement in front of a notary—the clerk at the courthouse. Then the victim is free to leave. A judge will review the victim's petition and sign the court order in a timely manner. This order will be delivered to the abuser, who is called the respondent.

In most states, no-contact orders have two parts: an immediate order (ex parte) that will take effect immediately and the order that is issued after a hearing. A copy of the order is also made available to the victim. The respondent may be given a few days to request a hearing before the temporary order goes into force for a longer period of time. If the respondent requests a hearing, some areas require the victim to attend the hearing at the same time as the abuser and some don't. If the victim is required to attend the hearing at the same time as the abuser, the victim can take any family member, witness, police officer, or victim's advocate to accompany her.

All conversations at the hearing will be between the judge and the victim (petitioner) or the judge and the abuser (respondent). The victim does not have any direct conversation or contact with the abuser. The victim may also ask a victim's advocate or police officer to speak for him or her. The respondent will be given an opportunity to make a statement. The victim will also be given a chance to add additional information not included in the paperwork, such as further harassment from the abuser. The judge has the victim's statement and any attachments to the court order, such as a past criminal record for the respondent. The judge will assess if there has been any contact made with the victim since the temporary court order went into effect. Then the judge will make a final decision, and the court order goes into effect for a specified period.

If the abuser disobeys the court order during this time, in some areas the court order will become binding for a lifetime. Criminal charges may also be filed. The abuser may also be arrested and prosecuted for any crime he has committed before, during, or after the time the court order is in effect. Each court has its own way of dealing with abuse issues where court orders are involved and criminal charges are filed. Victims should understand the legal process and find out what rights they have to get relief or protection from their abuser. Not knowing what to do or worrying about what will happen to them after they report abuse keeps far too many victims from using the law to protect themselves and their children.

Involving the legal system. Seriously harming or threatening to harm someone is a crime. Most states have mandatory reporting laws. It is important for all of us to educate ourselves about the legal process. Abuse will not stop unless the abuser is forced to be accountable for his or her actions. If we are abused, witness abuse, or suspect abuse, it is our duty to report it to a local law enforcement authority or social service agency. Information about reporting is available from the police or the government division of family services. If someone who is not the victim reports the abuse, they should be careful to use the victim's exact wording. A child's abuse account may be recorded so the child does not have to repeat it. Some states have compulsory treatment programs as an alternative to jail time. Victims should not feel guilty about initiating a court order, arrest, prosecution, or compulsory treatment for an abusive family member. That may be the only way to save those stuck in the abuse cycle.

The focus of involving the court is to resolve an abusive situation. If an offender is willing to take responsibility—as demonstrated through success in a recognized abuse evaluation and treatment program—the courts are more likely to grant the offender the opportunity to resolve the problem outside of jail.

When someone is arrested. If law enforcement officers are called to an abuse crime scene, they will try to separate those involved, ask questions, mediate the dispute, and then decide if a crime was committed. Officers generally gather statements and evidence; look for blood, torn clothing, grab marks, damaged furniture, and alcohol/drug containers; ask for a picture of the victim or the crime scene; and request the victim go to the emergency room and acquire X-rays or a doctor's exam. The police at the scene will also decide whether they will issue a citation or arrest the abuser. If cited, the abuser may be ordered to leave. If arrested, the abuser will go to jail. Some states have mandatory pro-arrest laws for family abuse crimes. This means the state makes the charge and doesn't require the victim to do so. This gives the victim time to get legal protection and hold the abuser accountable for the safety and well-being of all concerned.

PROVIDING SUPPORT FOR ABUSE VICTIMS

Those who desire to help should reassure victims they're doing the right thing when they report abuse. Reporting abuse by a family member may throw a victim into sheer panic or deep mourning. Reporting abuse means the victim has faced a reality he or she has hidden or postponed. Grieving a failed family relationship and facing an unknown life without the abuser can be frightening and intimidating. Victims need someone who is steady to stand by them through the process of reporting abuse, protecting themselves, and moving on with their lives. Victims are often threatened, convinced no one will believe them, or told they caused the abuse. Others are told horrible things will happen to a family member if they tell or that reporting will destroy the family. For that reason, most victims never tell anyone outside the family. When child abuse victims become adults, they're often so confused regarding their disturbed family unit that they endlessly try to solve family problems that grow larger over time. Reporting gives victims a chance to heal. Healing can't begin when abuse is kept secret, denied, minimized, dismissed, or ignored. If we know an abuser and if we love him or her, or if we love the victim, we should encourage them to set the accountability process in motion. Victims shouldn't shield abusers out of a mistaken sense of loyalty or love.

Victims often need the emotional and physical support of someone who is willing to literally stand next to them in the necessary but difficult process of reporting abuse to law enforcement and Church officials.

One woman described her first experience with the court system this way:

> While standing in a courtroom with a police officer to protect me from my abuser, I was shaking uncontrollably. I can't begin to tell you how much courage it took for me to finally put an end to the terrifying

physiological or physical threat my abuser held over my life. I spent the entire evening before my court appearance in bed, violently ill in absolute terror contemplating what awful thing might happen the next day. It is impossible to describe the sheer panic I felt when I finally stood up for myself because I knew my abuser was capable of any form of retaliation.

Those who desire to help also need to understand that some abuse victims still love their abusers. Separating themselves from their failed relationship is heartbreaking and difficult even when it is the right thing to do. Because abusers can be wonderful some of the time and awful only part of the time, victims are often conflicted about their choice to hold the abuser accountable. Those who want to help should tell the victims they don't have to stop loving the abuser, but they do have to stop the abuse and keep themselves safe from further abuse. The most loving act a victim can do for herself and for the abuser is to stop the abuse and hold the abuser accountable. It's important for leaders and friends to be a listening ear and a shoulder to cry on yet still help the victim face reality. One reality, demonstrated by statistical information and current research, is that abusers seldom change.

Abuse survivors who finally decide to report abuse are often in a state of abject fear or deep mourning that deserves tenderness and steadiness. Overly simplistic comments about how easy it "should be" to disentangle their unfulfilled dreams and get on with life are not helpful. Ending a relationship is never easy. Victims may need time to grieve. They also need a safe place to live away from the abuser while they are grieving and developing a plan for their future life free from abuse. Finally accepting that the abuser is not going to change and that the time and love invested in the relationship will not bear fruit is a tragedy much like a death in the family. The death of a family relationship while both people are still alive is often more complicated and heartbreaking than what happens when a family member actually does die. Victims have suffered a life-altering trauma.

If someone confides in you that they are being or have been abused, reassure her that the decision to tell you was right. Try to separate your needs from the victim's needs.

Some other suggestions for supporting abuse victims include:

- Listen carefully and allow the victim to share positive and negative feelings.
- Be objective and gather information.
- Help the victim create a positive plan of action.
- Limit the abuser's access to the victim.
- Don't deny the problem or blame the victim.
- Tell the victim you love her and that the abuser is the only one to blame.
- Don't withdraw affection from the victim or make outbursts toward the perpetrator.
- Don't make the event into a catastrophe or say the victim is damaged forever.
- Help the victim deal with irrational guilt, fear of rejection, and retaliation by the abuser.
- Provide victims with accurate information about healthy relationships.
- Help the abuse survivor maintain a normal routine without the abuser present.
- Provide reassurances to the other members in the family.

DATING PARTNER ABUSE

Dating partner abuse is also common. All young men and women should be educated and warned about predatory and abusive dating partners and instructed to resist and report any controlling, threatening, stalking, or inappropriate sexual behavior. The local law enforcement agency should have a victim's advocate to help those reporting abuse and seeking a no-contact order or stalking injunction from the courts.

One woman told me about a controlling dating partner who wouldn't take no for an answer. She was young, a year out of high school, and he was handsome, athletic, and charming. When he asked her to marry him three weeks after they met, she was flattered but had lingering doubts. She spoke to the young man's bishop before she gave her consent. The bishop told her the young man had had some moral problems in the past but assured her that they were resolved and he was temple worthy. So she agreed and after a short engagement they were sealed in the temple. After the wedding, he quickly resumed his immoral lifestyle and began abusing her physically, emotionally, and sexually.

"I wish I could tell every young person—take time to get to know the person you marry," she said. "Be aware that some people lie to their bishops to get a recommend. Just because someone has a temple recommend doesn't mean they are truly worthy. I stayed in that marriage because I'd always been taught that a temple marriage was forever, and I thought I was supposed to make it work no matter what. I almost lost my sanity and my life before I finally took my son and left. I'm now married to a good man and my children have a father who loves them and who treats us all with respect and kindness."

HOW TO BE SUPPORTIVE WHEN CHILDREN DISCLOSE ABUSE

Those concerned with the wellbeing of children should be aware of early childhood symptoms of abuse. Children often don't have the language or experience to understand what is happening to them. Children who are abused often display fear, anger, hostility, aggressive outbursts, anxiety, confusion, sleep disturbances, nightmares, bed wetting, social withdrawal, phobias, loss of appetite, and sexualized behavior. Other signs of early childhood abuse are bruises or scars, age regression, soiling underwear, night terrors, wide mood swings, suicidal thoughts or attempts, flashbacks, and split personalities. When children disclose abuse it is important to stay calm. Ask simple questions for clarification. Establish credibility and promise you will protect the victim from further abuse. Next, report the abuse to authorities and assess the overall effect of the abuse on the victim.

COMMON QUESTIONS OF CHILD VICTIMS

- Why did this happen to me? (I don't know. It was not your fault.)
- Why didn't you protect me? (I didn't know. Now that I know, I will.)
- What will happen to the abuser? (The abuser will be questioned and receive the consequences of his or her actions.)

- What will happen to me? (I will take you to a doctor. I will stay with you.)
- Am I bad? (You're not bad. What happened to you was wrong and against the law. Your abuser has a problem and will be stopped. They will not have any more access to you.)
- Are you mad at me because I let him or her do it? (No. I am not mad at you. Children don't consent; they obey.)

HELPING ADULTS WHO WERE ABUSED AS CHILDREN

Some individuals who were abused as children may not remember or tell others of the abuse until they are adults. Remembering will be traumatic. Many won't believe they forgot something so horrible. When someone discloses abuse, they need others to react with love. Our reaction to adult disclosures of past abuse can either help or harm those who confide in us. Here are some suggestions:

- Avoid making judgments about the accuracy of events.
- Be respectful, kind, and patient.
- Listen to their stories about abuse with compassion.
- Believe and support the victim.
- Encourage the victim to seek the aid of a professional therapist.
- Let the victim decide how much to share. Don't probe or prod.
- Keep confidences.
- Be a true friend.

One caution: Even though the vast majority of those who claim to be victims are honest and all legitimate victims are innocent, in rare cases, some people claim to be victims of abuse when in fact they are not. There is much controversy in the field of recovered memories.

HELPING SPOUSE ABUSE VICTIMS

Abuse victims often need help understanding that they are not breaking up the marriage or the family—abuse does that. Abuse violates all covenants and promises. It is not appropriate for priesthood leaders, friends, or family members to recommend divorce. That is a decision that must be prayerfully made between an individual and God. When we know that a person is being abused, we can help them gain perspective by giving them this information:

- Abuse is a crime and should be reported to legal authorities.
- Abuse victims should hold the offender responsible or the abuse will continue.
- Victims do not need to tolerate or endure abuse.
- Physiological, physical, and sexual assault is against the laws of the land and of God.
- Support or assistance is available from many sources, such as friends, bishops, professional counselors, LDS Family Services, police, or a social service agency.
- Safe houses, court orders, and legal assistance will provide distance and safety.
- Abusers seldom change.

FAMILY ABUSE

Family abuse typically affects victims more profoundly than abuse by strangers, because those who should love and protect us instead choose to hurt us. When strangers abuse us, we have loving arms to return to and a soft place to heal. Victims of violent and controlling abusers within their family may have to leave suddenly and secretly and go to a safe place where they can no longer be controlled or abused while they set in motion the protection of civil law. Other victims may stand up to the abuser, ask them to leave, seek counseling, and learn assertiveness skills. Some victims need the specific words to use when they confront their abuser. For instance, "I can no longer allow you to speak to me or treat me without respect and kindness. I will protect myself from now on. Your behavior is abusive. If this abuse continues, I will have to remove myself from our relationship and obtain protection."

In the April 1985 general conference, President Hinckley said, "A plague of child abuse [is] spreading across the world. Perhaps it has always been with us but has not received the attention it presently receives. I am glad that there is a hue and cry going up against this terrible evil, too much of which is found among our own. Fathers [and mothers], you cannot abuse your little ones without offending God. . . . Any man [or woman] who beats or in other ways abuses his [or her] children will be held accountable before the great judge of us all."[1]

Elder Richard G. Scott counseled: "Changing a profoundly embedded pattern of life can be very difficult. . . . Persistent faith in the Savior and obedience will see you through such hardships to greater blessings. The scriptures illustrate how conviction and faith can overcome traditions in conflict with God's plan, bringing blessings to individuals, and even generations of people."[2]

There is an army standing by to help all victims who seek out assistance. Yet abuse survivors must be willing to make difficult decisions before others can offer lasting help. The average victim returns many times to the abuser before gathering the courage to end the relationship. If we ask, God will give us the strength we need to stop the pain and move on with our lives.

We are never left alone or comfortless. All that is lost to us will be made up in God's time and in God's way. Christ extends His loving arms and offers this gentle reassurance for all of us: "Fear not, little children, for you are mine, and I have overcome the world, and you are of them that my Father hath given me; and none of them that my Father hath given me shall be lost" (D&C 50:41–42).

NOTES

1. Gordon B. Hinckley, "To Please Our Heavenly Father," *Ensign*, May 1985, 50.
2. Richard G. Scott, "Removing Barriers to Happiness," *Ensign*, May 1998, 86.

Chapter Eight

PRACTICAL GUIDANCE

There is a fundamental difference between a person who has been abused and someone who has not. The difference lies in the core way that person sees the world and themselves. Those who have been abused often see themselves as unworthy of love and doomed to painful relationships. They have learned that the world is not a safe place and people cannot be trusted. Those who have been abused by family members have learned that close relationships are frightening, unpredictable, dangerous, and painful.

On the other hand, someone who has not experienced abuse or trauma as a child has a greater opportunity to grow up feeling basically good about themselves and believing that the world is most often a safe place. If painful things happen to them, they know there will be a loving home to go back to and caring people around to support them and help them heal. That distinction might seem unimportant, but it is life-altering. This insight also helps those who desire to love and support victims but are confused by their behavior. Though we can never minimize the impact of abuse, we need to know there is always a way to heal and stop the pain from going to the next generation.

PROBLEMS AND BAGGAGE

There is an important difference between the problems of mortality and the baggage we pick up because of those problems. The problems of mortality happen to us through no fault of our own.

Those who are abused are given one of the greatest problems of mortality. Baggage, on the other hand, is the heavy load we carry around because of those problems. We can't always change the problems we have to deal with, but we can choose to leave personal baggage behind.

Many abuse survivors spend a lifetime searching for approval, success, love, and validation. Some seek wealth, notoriety, respect, or positions of power, while others turn to self-destructive behaviors—all in an effort to fill a deep inner sadness and need to be loved. Still others exhibit a façade of perfectionism and high achievement, yet inwardly feel like undiscovered frauds, undeserving of all their accomplishments. Why? The foundation of a child's self-image develops in the earliest years of life. That's why it's imperative we raise our children in loving security and never minimize the impact of any form of abuse. It's also important to remember that types of abuse should never be compared, for each child's response to abuse makes each case unique. The damage to a victim is serious, because an abused child has a hard time trusting God without loving earthly parents as role models. For that reason, seeking help from the only source that provides true love and healing is often left untapped.

NEGATIVE PATTERNS CAN CHANGE

If we were abused as children, we learned ways to protect ourselves. If we're still protecting ourselves in the same way, it isn't working anymore. Unhealed victims often project their unresolved issues with parents and siblings in the past onto their spouses and children in the present. In other words, we tend to make our spouses and children pay for the bad things our parents and siblings did to us. We can reprogram our thoughts and behavior so we can more clearly see the needs of those around us in the present. No mortal can eliminate our past or love us enough to make up for an abusive childhood—only God can. When we acknowledge, mourn, and heal from our past, we're free to leave it behind. If we remain unhealed—our past becomes our present. As we seek to heal, we'll discover patterns of thinking and behaving that need changing. A few of the most common negative patterns follow.

Those who have been abused often spend too much time listening to constant negative self-talk, repeating the kind of brainwashing they received as children. Negative thoughts feel like reality when, in fact, they are lies. Many victims resist changing their thought patterns because it challenges their distorted reality. Those who were abused as children learned early how to flip reality. If a child who has an abusive family member sees his life for what it is—a terrifying and unpredictable experience—he can't cope with getting out of bed every day. If, however, the child decides to see the abusive family member as good so he can survive, he must conclude he deserves the treatment he receives. As a result, those who have been abused grow up feeling constantly guilty—even though the guilt is irrational—and they often struggle with depression and low self-esteem. Many victims never feel good enough, no matter how hard they try to do what's right. Because they've learned to repress their feelings, many adults who were victimized as children have a hard time expressing emotions. Other victims can't seem to control their emotions and act out repeatedly with anger and rage.

Because they have past experiences with a family member who was abusive, some victims have strong negative feelings toward one sex. Because they experienced no power as children, many who were victimized as children also show a high need to be in control. Many abuse victims never feel safe. They live in a state of constant alertness and vigilance. Never knowing what awful experience to expect next, victims fear that any act or comment on their part may be used as an excuse for further abuse. This requires victims to be ever ready for the next assault.

Because close attachments or emotional connections in childhood brought only pain, victims learn to hold back and be suspicious of others' motives. Emotional connectedness with other people triggers feelings of fear and anxiety. Victims lack faith or trust in anyone because as children they couldn't trust those who should have loved them most. Victims experience overwhelming feelings of shame, confusion, worthlessness, and vulnerability. Many victims choose to remain aloof, believing that if others really knew them, they would be disgusted.

All negative and unproductive ways of thinking and behaving can be changed. The journey to healing requires faith, persistence, and courage. Discouragement in our efforts to eliminate these destructive thoughts and behaviors doesn't come from God. Our Father in Heaven wants us to recognize our weaknesses, and then he gives us the power to overcome them. God locks no one into any thought patterns or behavior with no way out. Alone, we're powerless. If we use our agency to draw on God's power and love, we don't need to feel discouraged in our efforts to change; rather, we can feel humble and reliant on the Savior.

Abuse is particularly harmful to those who live through it as children because they have not yet gained a true and healthy picture of themselves. Family abuse teaches children not to trust themselves, adults, or God. Abuse teaches a child that pain is to be expected from close relationships and there is no protection except denial or numbness. It teaches victims that their single purpose in life is to satisfy the needs of the abuser and that their own needs are not important. Abuse causes the victims to distrust their intuitive perception of reality. Abuse interferes with normal development and affects victims socially and in their roles as parents. Not only blatant abuse but also subtle abuse can accomplish these distortions. All forms of abuse profoundly affect victims.

Those who have been abused are more likely to abuse themselves. It's never acceptable to tear ourselves down. It's important to admit to our faults and weaknesses, but it's also important to have compassion for ourselves. For example, once when an old friend approached me, I hardly recognized her. She'd lost several hundred pounds and her countenance shone. She smiled as she threw her arms around me and whispered that my love for her had changed her life. Of course, it was obvious to me that she had changed her own life. Then she tearfully thanked me for loving her. She said that she'd felt respect and love from me that had caused her to reexamine her own beliefs about herself. She began to understand that if I could find her worthwhile and lovable, perhaps God could feel the same way. This remarkable woman realized she'd spent her whole adult life abusing herself in the same way her parents and siblings had abused her as a child. Her self-abuse consisted of self-loathing thoughts and self-destructive behaviors. She decided she was sick and tired of being sick and tired and determined she was ready to change.

It all started with her thoughts. Whenever a fearful or self-defeating thought entered her head, she replaced it with a hopeful, grateful, or self-affirming thought. She made a list of positive quotes and carried it around with her. With her newly discovered inner sense of value, she told her parents and siblings she expected them to treat her with respect. Some of her family members improved their behavior toward her and others didn't. She made a decision to no longer put herself in harm's way. She told me that the better she felt about herself on the inside, the less likely she was to do something to hurt herself on the outside, such as overeating, depending on drugs to ease pain, or not exercising. Her outward and inward transformation was astounding.

TAKING ACTION

It's important for victims to understand that what happened to them was not their fault, but how they respond in the present is their responsibility. Those who have been abused have the responsibility to do the following:

- Evaluate what happened to them as children and what is happening today.
- Become aware of the negative influences past abuse has on current behavior.
- Make sure all current relationships are respectful.
- Ask God for an increased understanding of how to more fully live the gospel.
- Develop a plan to learn and practice the skills for healthy relationships.
- Utilize community and Church resources to break the abuse cycle.
- Never give up hope in themselves, others, and the Atonement.

Many unhealed abuse survivors haven't experienced any real control over their lives and, as a result, have not fully discovered their own personal power. They often exhibit a strong need to be in control of outward appearances to mask an out-of-control and painful inner life. What unhealed abuse survivors don't understand is that outward appearances and controlling others is not power and does not provide the security they desperately seek. Outward or other control is the opposite of personal power.

Healing from abuse is a long, hard journey, but it is possible to have a wonderful and fulfilling life if we climb out of the hole we've been put in and decide to provide for someone else what we didn't receive. Instead of focusing on what we didn't get, we focus on what we have to give.

For example, one woman told me she couldn't understand her driving need to keep her house excessively clean or why she struggled with anorexia. It wasn't until she felt the pain of and healed from her childhood abuse that she was given insight into her own behavior. Her physically violent mother had traumatized her as a child. Her sexually abusive father had given her a distorted view of herself and the beauty of human intimacy. The only thing she could control as a child was how much she ate and how clean she kept her bedroom. These obsessive habits helped her feel some sense of control then but were blocking her growth as an adult. She felt immense pressure to appear perfect to people in her church and neighborhood. She thought if anyone really knew her, they would be disgusted. She was unable to relax and often suffered with anxiety attacks and chronic health problems.

This woman described her journey to healing this way:

> When I gained the insight that my whole life was a reaction to my abusive childhood, I was able to move forward. I still struggle with thoughts of self-hatred, but now I know I have a choice. I can choose to replace those thoughts and I can choose how I behave. Now I realize the Savior is there to help me. I had to end my relationship with my parents completely and surround myself with loving people and activities that keep me growing and learning. I also discovered that the guilt I thought I was feeling from severing my relationship with my parents was actually fear and longing. I feared more hurt and punishment from my parents because of my decision and I longed for the happy, loving family I would never have. Now I focus on the good life I can create and the people I can love. Now I face life's challenges and appreciate my blessings and opportunities.

Survivors of abuse need help experiencing true power, which comes after learning to have faith and trust in our identity as children of God and fully receiving the gift of the Atonement of Jesus Christ. Personal power comes when we understand that we don't have to be in control of events, other people, or outward appearances, because God is already in control and always uses power in righteous ways. As we heal from abuse, we begin to understand for the first time that we live in a basically safe world. We can let go of fears and our need to be in control because we've learned to trust God. We learn to actively encourage our own, our spouse's, and our children's independence. We slowly develop an inner awareness that we can survive whatever happens to us because we're filled with God's love and we trust Him. We have no great fears dominating our thoughts and behavior. With a new awareness of true personal power, those who choose to heal from abuse develop a new understanding of the sanctity of their own souls that expands to the sanctity of every soul.

EFFECTIVE THERAPY

Those who have been abused may be assisted through the healing process with professional counseling. Each person seeking an effective counselor should carefully shop around until they've found someone who matches their needs and value system. A therapist-client relationship should be open, accepting, and empathetic. An effective counselor should help those who have been abused to do the following:

Accept the reality of past abuse without minimization or denial. This acceptance shouldn't depend on validation by others. Family members may still deny what happened or minimize its effect. Victims should be taught to trust their feelings.

Give up responsibility for the abuse. The victim's natural need for love and attention was exploited to serve the impulses of the abuser. In many cases, the victim was too young to understand abuse or lacked the necessary information to stop the abuse.

Break the cycle of secrecy. A good counselor will help the victim understand that secrecy will not protect the well-being of the family. Secrecy encourages abuse to continue. It takes courage to bring up matters other family members want to minimize, ignore, or deny.

Grieve a lost childhood. Victims often live with an overwhelming feeling of sadness. A family where abuse has taken place is sick, and the love expressed is a sham if the abuse is known and no action is taken. In such circumstances, the parents do not love or protect their children. Victims who disclose abuse are blamed for disrupting the family. Isolation and shame are overwhelming. A good therapist can help the victim deal with all these emotions.

Deal constructively with the pain of abuse. Victims often bury their feelings and never feel sad or happy. Some try to be invisible, while others try to forget by abusing substances.

Learn to feel again. Male victims of abuse tend to turn their anger and rage outward, and female victims tend to turn the anger and rage inward. Feelings of anger, rage, and bitterness often mask pain, sadness, and grief.

Nurture the inner child. Abuse survivors need help relearning how to live joyfully and should be guided to find their personal passion by doing a variety of things like exploring nature, reading uplifting books, learning a musical instrument, writing, experimenting with a new hobby, or serving others.

Practice assertive skills. Assertiveness training includes seeing others as equals. The ability to state what you want is difficult for abuse survivors. Many abuse survivors lack the ability to know their own needs.

Learn to give personal health habits a high priority. Taking good care of self is often something that abuse survivors neglect.

Relearn the meaning of healthy personal boundaries. Abuse survivors often have a difficult time providing security, respect, and privacy for themselves.

Understand normal, healthy sexual intimacy without exaggerating or denying the place of sexual feelings.

Learn to use spiritual resources like personal prayer, study of the scriptures, and Church leaders' advice for healing.

Recognize past abuse does not have to control present identity. Many victims feel they are forever damaged goods. That is a lie.

Find ways to help others with empathy and understanding. Those who have experienced abuse are better able to understand and empathize with other victims.

Become open, honest, and loving. Abuse survivors have learned to survive by closing off their feelings. They need guidance to open their hearts again.

Recognize present situations that are abusive. It takes a retraining of old habits to recognize abusive situations and relationships.

Regain self-esteem and trust. Those who survive abuse need to relearn who they are and find at least one person they can completely trust.

REPROGRAMMING OUR BRAIN

The way we are parented in childhood programs our brain into patterns of thinking and reasoning. If we have been taught to think in negative or fearful ways, that mode of thinking may have become a habit—but it is one that can be reprogrammed. We can effectively rewire our way of thinking to be more positive. One way to replace negative thinking is to constantly think about what we're grateful for. Grateful thoughts help us see life with more clarity. It also helps to write down all our blessings in a journal.

Another way to rewire our brains is to regularly repeat positive statements that help us move forward into the future with hope. Positive and self-affirming thoughts repeated over and over have the ability to effectively rewire our brains with new connections. We can't control what thoughts enter our heads, but we can control whether they stay. We can replace negative or fearful thoughts with positive and life-affirming ones. Each person needs to thoughtfully choose his own affirming statements and reprogram negative thinking patterns. Here are some examples of positive statements. Note that they are both first person and present tense.

I am a child of God.
I accept myself.
I will not hide my feelings or disguise my hurt.
When I feel upset, I call on God to help me return to inner peace and calm.
I choose to let go of all the things I can't control or change.
I choose to forgive myself and others out of strength, not weakness.

I am properly rested, I eat regular and nutritious meals, and I exercise.

I allow myself time for useful work, friendships, and spontaneous play.

I choose to conserve my energy for things that really matter to me.

I value, appreciate, and share the gifts God has given me.

I listen to my body and my spirit and sense what I need.

I seek out friends and places that are nourishing and uplifting.

I let go of harsh expectations and unrealistic demands for myself and others.

I feel good wishes coming my way from all those who care about me.

I am surrounded by love and by those who offer me strength and comfort.

I am strong and courageous enough for whatever God wants me to do.

My body and spirit are strong and resilient.

I have gifts to share, a purpose in life, and people to serve.

There are hidden treasures to be discovered from the pain of my past.

I am not afraid. God is with me and strengthens me.

I have a divine spirit of infinite worth.

With God at my side, I am strong enough to face anything life throws at me.

I see beauty and strength in myself and others and in the world around me.

I love my body as a precious gift from God to assist me on my mortal journey.

I honor my courage to grow after I have experienced difficult circumstances.

As I release my grief and pain, I hold my love in a different way.

The pain I have endured softens my heart and adds to my wisdom and compassion.

HOPEFUL THOUGHTS

All emotion begins with a thought. If we don't like what we're feeling, it helps to go back and pay attention to what thought preceded that feeling. Our emotions function as the oil gauge of our spirits. Like the "check engine" light that comes on in a car when something is wrong with the engine, our emotions should warn us that something's not working with our thinking. When we see the oil light on the dashboard, we have a choice to inspect the engine and determine the oil level or to ignore that warning light. If we ignore the oil light, we'll experience a major vehicle breakdown. If we ignore our negative and fearful thoughts, we can experience a major spiritual breakdown. We have the power to label our negative or fearful thoughts and replace them with positive and peaceful ones. We actually shape our brain by the thoughts we think, just as we shape our muscles when we exercise. When we have a negative or fearful thought, we are using the primitive regions of our brain instead of the frontal cortex, where we are able to process higher-level thinking skills.

This is the scenario most of us generally follow. First, something happens to us; then we have a thought; then we experience an emotion. For instance, let's say someone does something we consider offensive. We immediately have a negative or fearful thought about that person. Suddenly we feel angry, afraid, or insulted. Those emotions result from that first, almost unconscious, negative thought, not necessarily from the offensive behavior.

Even when we have a negative thought initially, we can choose to immediately replace it with a more hopeful one. After a hopeful thought, our resulting emotion might be pity or even compassion for the person who was unkind to us. Once we become aware of our negative or fearful thoughts, we have the choice to replace them by asking ourselves, "What is a more hopeful way to think about this?" We access great personal power during that space of time between when something happens to us and when we choose our response. The first response is always a thought, which becomes an emotion and then a behavior. When we fully realize the opportunity we have to label and change our thoughts and subsequent responses to any life circumstance, we unlock the awesome power of individual choice.

Many abuse survivors have developed negative thinking patterns that involve critical or negative thoughts about self or others. We need to pay attention to our negative thoughts if we want to change them into a more hopeful way of thinking and fill our minds with these kinds of thoughts:

> I am a valuable person.
> I trust myself to make good choices.
> I am unique.
> It's okay to make a mistake.
> I don't have to be perfect all the time.
> I can express my true feelings.
> I have a wide range of talents and abilities.
> I am attractive and likable.
> There are healthy people for me to love.
> I am a capable person.
> I can make my life better.
> Success comes in small steps.
> I can laugh at myself.
> I am a precious child of God.

CHANGING THE NATURAL MAN

To become like our Heavenly Parents, we have to let go of the natural man (see Mosiah 3:19) and selfishness, even if that selfishness is manifest in self-hatred. Both self-hatred and self-aggrandizement are types of self-absorption. Self-absorption blocks our connection to heaven. The Holy Ghost has a difficult time communicating with someone who has a mind full of hate. Comparing ourselves to others leads to either self-intolerance or pride. Self-hatred leads to depression, fear of trying new things, and constant nitpicking about our faults to the point of despair. Self-despair leads us to attack ourselves and feel like failures when we make mistakes. Both self-hatred and pride keep us from God's love and enlightenment about our own and others' true nature and eternal potential. They keep us blind to the knowledge that we and others are unique, incomparable, beloved children of God.

When we allow pride or self-hatred to take over, we become abusive to others or ourselves. We put ourselves first instead of God. We become self-absorbed, self-concerned, self-aggrandizing, self-hating, or self-centered. When we are self-deceived, we bring blindness, resentment, despair, misery, and cynicism to all our relationships, including our relationship with God and ourselves.

Can we honestly say, "I will give away all my sins to know thee" (Alma 22:18)—including self-hatred? God knows us as we really are, naked and undisguised. He knows every hidden part of us, every bad thing we've done, and He still loves us, wants us—all of us. Each soul is precious to God. When our will becomes one with the will of our Father in Heaven, we no longer need to struggle. We have only to be ourselves, made whole through the atoning blood of Jesus Christ. When we give our hearts to God, we dedicate our lives to becoming an instrument of peace and love.

Section Three

HOW TO OVERCOME
THE EFFECTS OF ABUSE

Chapter Nine

BREAKING FREE FROM
DESTRUCTIVE FAMILY PATTERNS

Any family tradition or pattern of behavior that leads us to disrespect ourselves or others must be changed. We are not breaking the commandment to honor our parents when we refuse to be part of abusive family interactions. Children often struggle to look objectively at their parent's actions. Yet, transcending the restrictive aspects of our heritage is vital to our growth.

The pull most of us have to our parents no matter how they treat us is strong, but we must understand that abuse is a web that traps and harms both of us. We need to be honest about what we are up against and remove ourselves from all abusive relationships. We need to understand that love and acceptance from abusers is not possible. The reason abused children become abusive adults is that they haven't become objective about their parents' behavior. Our response to a bad childhood often determines our perspective and behavior as adults.

One woman described the atmosphere in her home as a child this way:

> I used to wet the bed. When I told my mother about an accident, I was hit, shamed, and forced to sleep in the soiled bed. So I hid my wet underwear under my bed and slept on the floor. I used to rock and sing to myself over and over at night so that I wouldn't fall asleep and have another accident. I was so ashamed of myself, I wanted to

curl up in a tiny ball and disappear. Carefully and methodically, I was taught that I didn't matter. I wasn't a living, breathing child with a broken heart—I was a prop, a piece of scenery designed to give the audience staring at the stage of my family the impression of a reality that didn't exist. My purpose in life was to make my parents look good to others outside our home. If I didn't play my part in the façade well, painful consequences followed. I remember the eyes of my siblings watching when I was belittled or whipped, staring at me with blank expressions. I realize now they couldn't come to my aid without putting themselves at risk. Now I know forcing a child to witness abuse can be as damaging as being the victim. When I got married, I prayed every single day and asked God to help me know how to love my husband and children. The impressions I received were directive about how I needed to change my self-loathing thoughts. Slowly, I was able to see my childhood objectively and make a choice to raise my family differently.

Those who are abused as children are painfully isolated. No one clothes them with beautiful truths about themselves or dresses them with comforting reassurances about the world around them. No eyes light up when they walk into the room. All the pain of being unloved is buried deep inside. Abuse victims believe the destructive lies they're told. Helpless, shamed, and stripped of human dignity, children who are abused live in constant fear and humiliation. If the only time you're given positive attention is when you do something to make your parents look good, you begin to play their game. Soon you don't see the truth or act in your own best interest, eventually losing awareness of your own needs. Childhood abuse victims are often not even aware they've been seduced into secrecy.

The following account is how one woman described when she realized she could ask for help outside her abusive family:

> I was eighteen before the thought even entered my head that I could call someone outside my family to help me during an abusive family situation. I thought all families were like mine. I'd been waiting for a ride home from work for several hours outside on a freezing December night. All of my family members had gone to bed and forgotten about me. I walked to a girl friend's apartment, woke her, and asked if I could use the telephone to call home for a ride. When my brother finally arrived to pick me up, he quickly

flew into a violent rage and shoved me from the moving car onto the road in front of a hotel at 2:00 a.m. I walked into the hotel for shelter as my sibling sped away. Once I was inside the hotel, several intoxicated old men in the lobby propositioned me. If I called home or waited for my brother to come back, my situation would get worse. I prayed.

A clear directive flashed through my mind to call a friend. Even after being called out of bed in the middle of the night, my friend quickly arrived, put his arm around me, and drove me home. I thanked him for the ride without offering an explanation. I had nowhere else to go but back home because my father had taken all the money I'd earned so I could move out. I didn't dare ask Dad to return the money because I was always trying to please my parents. I'd lost the ability to know what I needed, let alone the will to ask for it. Now I understand when we try to please others instead of God, we lose our true identity or our unique self, who exists as a royal child of divine parentage.

One man described the atmosphere in his childhood home this way:

> Some of my siblings hid in their bedrooms when our parents were screaming at each other behind their locked bedroom door while others listened with our ears pressed against the lock. Once my sister broke open their bedroom door and screamed for them to stop. With so much continual contention, it was impossible to ever truly relax or feel safe. Because of my childhood, I determined that I would never put my own children through that ordeal. The greatest gift I can give my children it to love their mother.

Another man reflected on the lingering effects of childhood abuse this way:

> Once, while sitting in a restaurant, I realized why I always asked to be seated in the far corner of the serving room with my back against the wall, close to an exit. I was repeating a pattern of behavior I'd learned as a child to protect myself. With the violent and explosive tempers in my family, I never knew what was going to happen next. I was often hit from behind or trapped in a room with no quick exit. So I developed an unconscious habit of defensively positioning myself in a room to protect me from unexpected attacks and provide a quick exit. I also noticed I became overly anxious whenever my

wife left the house without telling me where she was going. I'd grown up with people who unexpectedly left our home in a rage and stayed away for days, years, or a lifetime. My wife's unannounced leaving triggered irrational fear inside me because of my past. Once I was aware of this baggage, I took my fears to the Savior. It took time, but today I live with an abiding sense of peace.

A family should be a refuge from the world. Healthy parents love their children simply because they exist; the child does not have to do anything to deserve or earn that love. Unhealthy parents have little or no true love to offer their children. They offer acceptance only when the child does what the parents want them to do. Those abused as children may find they need to leave home to create a healthy, loving home.

I live out in the country where, because of insufficient rainfall, we receive water for our fields in large irrigation ditches. My family property happens to be at the end of the ditch. If the owners of the fields upstream don't keep their ditches in good repair, an adequate volume of water does not get down the ditch far enough to effectively water our parched land. As a result, we have been limited with what we can do with our property. Likewise, parents who haven't repented, forgiven, and learned how to love leave the gaps open in their lives so their children are left with precious little water downstream to help them grow into loving people.

THE IMPORTANCE OF LOVING HOMES

What we learn about the ways of the world is first determined by what we experience in our families. What happens in our homes is more important than what happens in palaces, on battlefields, or in great halls of government. Our behavior in our home may have more impact for good or evil than anything else we do in our lives. We make our most sacred, voluntary covenants in this life with God and members of our family. President Howard W. Hunter said, "The family is the most important unit in time and in eternity and, as such, transcends every other interest in life."[1]

The love we offer our family may be the most important work we will ever do. Our greatest joys and sorrows are most often the result of family relationships. "An eternal bond doesn't just happen as a result of sealing covenants we make in the temple. How we conduct ourselves in this life will determine what we will be in all the eternities to come. To receive the blessings of the sealing that our Heavenly Father has given to us, we have to keep the commandments and conduct ourselves in such a way that our families will want to live with us in the eternities."[2]

The importance and priority parents give their families will literally determine the future course of mankind. President Spencer W. Kimball warned: "Many of the social restraints which in the past have helped to reinforce and to shore up the family are dissolving and disappearing. The time will come when only those who believe deeply and actively in the family will be able to preserve their families in the midst of the gathering evil around us."[3] There is no neutral ground in the universe. The battle over good and evil has already been won as a result of the War in Heaven and through the Atonement. Yet a vital battle still remains—the battle for the individual soul. There is nothing as important.

Our character is forged in the furnace of an ongoing personal battle to discern good from evil. "The greatest battle of life is fought out within the *silent chambers* of the soul."[4] The opportunity to exercise moral agency is a gift from a loving Creator who wants us to inherit all he has. Daily, hourly, we stand at the fork in the road and decide between light and darkness, pride or humility, good or evil, love or selfishness, our own will or God's. We can refuse God's love or accept it.

The most important decision we will ever make in this life is whether we will accept or reject the Atonement of our Lord and Savior Jesus Christ—and then live according to covenants that enable us to partake of the blessings. As we feel God's love, we develop an increased capacity to make decisions about our behavior, with more and more awareness of the eternal significance of our actions. God knows what brings His children growth, peace, and joy. So we're given loving directions called commandments to follow as a guide on our journey through mortality. Yet God leaves us free to choose, typically intervening in our lives only at our request and almost always only to help and heal. God creates, blesses, enlarges, empowers, uplifts, enlightens, and loves us. Though we will all be pierced by evil, if we turn to the Savior, a way is provided for us to repent, forgive, and heal.

RECOGNIZING AND STOPPING DESTRUCTIVE FAMILY PATTERNS

One roadblock to eliminating abuse is our desire to retain a family relationship at all costs. If abuse is tolerated, the relationship has already failed. There is still hope, but only if the abuse stops. Think of this dilemma another way: If neither person in an abusive relationship ever sees the abuser's behavior as wrong, the relationship will never be right. We have the responsibility to protect ourselves and our children from harm. We must not reward evil by continuing a relationship with those who abuse us. Real goodness stands between innocents and those who would harm them. Real goodness has the courage to leave behind all dangerous and destructive relationships.

Our choice to end abusive relationships is often made more difficult by relatives who disagree with our perceptions and actions. Just because others disagree with our choice does not mean it is wrong. People are largely driven by self-interest. Abusers will feed the self-doubt of the victim by telling them that they are the bad guy, are not honoring their parents, or are breaking up the marriage. In fact, the victim's choice to end an abusive relationship may be the only way to save the next generation.

When parents don't love God or each other, their children become objects who are defined by their parents' needs, forced to deal with dysfunctional marriages, and left to cope with upsetting matters over which they had no control. Parents must be willing to suffer and change to meet their children's needs. If parents choose not to repent and forgive, their children pay the price. If parents don't love their children, they need to work on themselves. Parents who are unable or unwilling to love their children were almost always unloved children themselves. Facing the reality of a parent's inability to love us can help us look more closely at what we are offering our own children. One way to honor our parents is to improve upon what they were able to offer us.

Adults can decide whether to have a guarded, limited, or no-contact arrangement with an abusive family member, but children have no choice. They are literally trapped in a toxic home environment, and the effects are disastrous. When parents don't love, respect, and forgive each other, they actively poison their children. When parents openly or subtly criticize or disparage each other to their children—whether it's true or not and whether they eventually get divorced or not—they give their children an impossible task to deal with. A child is part of each parent, and hating one means hating part of themselves.

Children of toxic marriages have no safe place to grow and develop because they're too busy taking care of Mom and Dad's problems. The parents are too wrapped up in themselves to fill the child's innate needs to be loved, accepted, valued, validated, and nurtured. No matter what the problems are in the marriage, the innocent child always suffers most.

Children learn what they live with. When a child lives with chaos, they learn confusion. If they live with violence, they learn insecurity and fear. If they live with abuse, they learn hatred of self and others. These children of abuse grow into adults forever masking their nakedness to compensate for feelings of loneliness and worthlessness. Parents who don't love each other or their children confuse their offspring about divine love.

Because children of abuse have experienced unhealthy substitutes for love, they often waste their lives unsuccessfully searching for someone or something to make them feel good about themselves, to help them feel worthy, acceptable, important, and nurtured. Ultimately, only God can fully provide those needs.

Siblings learn to work through differences with each other by observing their parents. If husbands and wives deal lovingly with their differences, they teach their children good habits that can last for generations. Elder Robert D. Hales counseled: "It helps children to see that good parents can have differing opinions, and that these differences can be worked out without striking, yelling, or throwing things. They need to see and feel calm communication with respect for each other's viewpoints so they themselves will know how to work through differences in their own lives."[5]

Some children grow up never experiencing healthy physical affection—never being hugged, kissed, or stroked. Many have never known what it feels like to have a gentle hand on their cheek or a strong, loving hand placed on their shoulder. Others never hear the words, "I love you" spoken in their home. Too many spouses hear constant criticism and verbal barrages about their failings. Far too often, children are ignored or neglected while parents battle it out in a constant marital war. Numerous children are used and abused sexually by parents or siblings. Some spouses and children are physically assaulted in the name of discipline. Others never receive sympathy or encouragement. Many are controlled by the volatile mood swings of family members. Most of this behavior was learned in childhood from parents who were unable or unwilling to teach their children what it means to love and be loved. We all behave in ways that feel normal to us.

When abusive families face a problem, they fight with each other instead of pulling together and trying to solve the problem. Family members with a history of abusive behavior try to dominate each other, only interact when they want something, and often cast all family conflicts in terms of victims, villains, and heroes. When one family member believes another is a villain, it prevents that person from seeing his or her part in family problems. This distorted view will also give that person an excuse for attempts to control. Control is the first desire of those who exercise unrighteous influence.

When family problems are recycled instead of solved, an ingrained and unhealthy pattern of relationships is the cause. When a family feud is going on, it helps to step back and refuse to join in. Ask, "Since everybody involved in this conflict is a member of the family, is there really an enemy here?" When the shooting begins, we're all wounded. When you think you're the hero in the family, you are more apt to believe your role is to punish somebody. When you think you're the victim, you're prone to feel powerless.

One of the most common unhealthy patterns in family relationships is triangulating, which happens when one family member has a problem or concern with another person in the family but goes to a third person in the family to complain. Problems are not solved in any relationship if individuals go to third parties hoping to find sympathy or support. Misunderstanding and miscommunication often escalate when the two individuals involved are not able to work out their differences between them. This pattern is especially harmful when individuals in a marriage relationship go to their children with their private marital problems. The child who is made a confidant is unable to resolve a problem he did not cause. Healthy families refuse to play the third-party game and direct problems in any relationship back to the two people involved.

We don't have to take sides when family members are fighting. If we do, we will deprive ourselves of much that is valuable in life in order to stay in step with other family members who are choosing negative, empty lives. Someone has to break from the multigenerational negativity and recognize their family relationship patterns are not taking them where they want to go—then choose a different road. Our decision to remove ourselves from negative family patterns will positively affect our family for generations.

One man expressed how he changed his longing for earthly parental love to his knowledge of his heavenly parents' love:

> I spent most of my life working hard, overachieving, and bending over backward in an effort to receive that elusive love and acceptance I longed for from my parents. Now I see those attempts as desperate and sad because I was always failing in their eyes. Because I idealized my parents, and because they did not truly love me, for years it was difficult to believe that I was lovable. I have since sought for and received assurances of divine love.

AFTER ALL WE CAN DO

Giving up the wish that the past can be different is discovering the hope that the future can be better. There is something sacred that compensates for all our sorrow. In our private, heartfelt desires, we often hope for the ideal outcome of family life, but no family is perfect. God knows our hearts. The Atonement of Jesus Christ will make up the difference, after all we can do. "He healeth the broken in heart, and bindeth up their wounds" (Psalm 147:3). The heaviest burden in life to carry is sin, both our own and that of others. We will find the answers to life's most painful questions through the

Atonement of our Lord and Savior. Christ always lovingly beckons, "Come unto me, all ye that labour and are heavy laden, and I will give you rest. Take my yoke upon you, and learn of me; for I am meek and lowly in heart: and ye shall find rest unto your souls" (Matthew 11:28–29).

Jesus Christ will not fail us. If we choose to continue repenting and forgiving, we will eventually be filled with peace and joy. "Ye cannot behold with your natural eyes, for the present time, the design of your God concerning those things which shall come hereafter, and the glory which shall follow after much tribulation. For after much tribulation come the blessings. Wherefore the day cometh that ye shall be crowned with much glory" (D&C 58:3–4). Christ will cover our nakedness, clothe us in immortality, and grant us eternal life through the power of His redeeming love.

NOTES

1. Howard W. Hunter, "Being a Righteous Husband and Father," *Ensign*, Nov. 1994, 50.
2. Robert D. Hales, "The Eternal Family," *Ensign*, Nov. 1996, 65.
3. Spencer W. Kimball, "Families Can Be Eternal," *Ensign*, Nov. 1980, 4.
4. Quoted by David O. McKay, in *Conference Report*, April 1969, 95.
5. Robert D. Hales, "How Will Our Children Remember Us?" *Ensign*, Nov. 1993, 9.

Chapter Ten

ABUSE AND THE
MARRIAGE RELATIONSHIP

Many LDS spouses have the mistaken idea they must tolerate abuse because their temple covenants compel them to endure whatever situation they live in forever. Others believe they are being forgiving if they stay in an abusive marriage. The Church takes a conservative stance regarding divorce and the cancellation of the temple sealing so members will take their covenants seriously. Leaders of the Church rightfully encourage spouses to work hard at their relationships and get all the help they need to save a sick marriage. But no one should conclude that Church leaders or doctrine require men or women in abusive relationships to stay together to preserve the sanctity of marriage. If that were the case, the Church would be an institutionalized defender of abuse, and that is simply never the case.

One woman described her parents' mutually abusive marriage this way:

> When I was a child, I cowered in the basement furnace room listening to my parents violently argue or battle it out physically. Hour after hour, year after year, decade after decade they fought about the same issue. Dad accused Mom of being unfaithful, and Mom accused Dad of being unfaithful with sordid and disturbing screaming matches. Listening to and witnessing their mutual dark

allegations and physical assaults left me feeling constantly terrified and nauseous, as if I were struggling for air while sinking to the bottom of the sea. I had constant stomach aches, always afraid of what was going to happen next. But mostly I felt like I must be the problem. If I didn't exist, my parents would be happy. When I got married I vowed not to repeat their legacy. Every night I knelt and asked God to teach me how to love my husband. Then I tried to follow the impressions I received. I am in a genuinely loving marriage today and our mutual respect has given all our children a safe place to grow.

One woman told me she experienced daily beatings by her alcoholic father while she was growing up. When the first opportunity to marry came along, she jumped at the chance.

"I knew my boyfriend had a bad temper, but it didn't seem as bad as my dad's," she said. "Things got ugly real fast. I stayed in a horrible marriage, because I thought that was the best I could do. Now my son is in jail, and my daughter is trapped in an abusive marriage. I thought I was being forgiving. Instead, I taught my daughter how to be a victim and my ex-husband taught my son how to be an abuser. I should have provided a safe home for all of us. I'm working very hard to change my life. I want to give my grandchildren a new model to follow. Because of Jesus, I know there is hope for all of us."

ABUSE IS A COVENANT BREAKER

Church doctrine consistently condemns abuse. Yet there are still those who don't understand that serious abuse is a violation of the sealing covenant and marriage vow and absolutely incompatible with gospel teachings. It is incorrect for Church members to believe their temple covenants compel them to endure a seriously abusive situation forever. Abuse is not a challenge designed to test our endurance. Patience, long-suffering, and hope are qualities that are helpful when problems in a marriage flow from differences in personalities, gender, and temperaments. These same positive qualities harm a family when abuse is being tolerated. Far too many couples don't realize how much they're hurting themselves and their children when their home is a war zone. Before long, children grow up and the damage has been done to the next generation.

In many marriages, the spouse of an abusive mate will tolerate cruel behavior in the belief they're holding the family together for the sake of the children. In truth, their failure to provide a safe, nurturing, loving home will damage every member of the family. The only way to guarantee the continuation of an eternal family is when all members are repenting and forgiving. We cannot have a celestial relationship with someone who is living a lesser law. Couples who believe that the abuse being tolerated in their marriage will affect only the two of them are sowing the wind and will later reap the whirlwind as they witness the damage in their posterity for years to come.

One woman expressed how she changed the legacy she'd been given this way:

> After we married, our visits to our parents' homes left my husband and me feeling so discouraged. Without a role model for a happy marriage, we wondered if there was any hope for us and understood we both had a lot to learn. So we got down on our knees and asked God to teach us. We profoundly mourned our parents' unhappy marriages and did not want to repeat their legacy for our children. We understood the greatest gift we had to offer our posterity was our abiding love for God and each other. We're not perfect, but we do love each other.

UNCOVERING UNHEALTHY MARRIAGE PATTERNS

All marriages have multiple challenges and problems. Some challenges come from outside the relationship and some from within. Healthy couples acknowledge, deal with, and work through their problems, or they amicably agree to disagree. Unhealthy couples ignore, deny, and blame their problems on their spouse, or they coexist in a never-ending war. When children grow up in a home where their parents are always fighting, they mature into love-starved adults. These needy adults carry childhood love-deprivation into all their relationships, especially with their future spouse and children. This lack of love and nurturing in childhood creates a needy adult who wastes a great deal of life attempting to fill an inner emptiness with substances, possessions, power, positions, or experiences that ultimately disappoint and never satisfy.

Though we can't go back and change anything, we can examine our childhood home environments and acknowledge any unhealthy patterns in our parents' relationship. After we analyze our parents' weaknesses and strengths, we can determine to create a relationship with our spouse that doesn't repeat the weaknesses, and then focus forward by actively practicing more positive relationship patterns so we won't pass along the same mistakes. Our children don't need that extra load; we will inadvertently pass along enough of our own mistakes.

IS IT EVER RIGHT TO DIVORCE?

Are there circumstances when the continuation of a marriage is a greater evil than divorce? Yes. Abuse is often one of those circumstances. Because the Church places a high priority on the marriage relationship, many couples are hesitant to disclose problems or get help when they live in abusive situations. Yet the most loving thing we can do for an abusing spouse who refuses to change her behavior is to hold her accountable.

If there is ongoing abuse in our marriage, we should immediately seek help. Because it is very difficult to act alone to stop cruel behavior from our spouse, those who are abused need help from someone outside the family. There are priesthood leaders, friends, officers of the law, and social service professionals standing by who are willing to give aid, education, comfort, and protection.

Some individuals have the mistaken idea that the person who initiates a divorce is breaking up a marriage. It is abuse that destroys a marriage, not the man or woman who decides to leave an abusive relationship. Most abusers never change, and it is not possible to have a healthy and loving relationship with them. It is not charitable to endlessly endure abuse. Spouses are not being loving or forgiving when they allow their mate to diminish their divine worth and hinder their God-given agency.

Abused spouses are not helping their mate by refusing to hold them accountable. Neither love nor loyalty requires a spouse to endure abuse. On the contrary, love and loyalty require married companions to put an end to all abusive behavior. When both spouses demonstrate a willingness to repent and forgive, there is always hope for the marriage. When one or both spouses refuse to repent and forgive, hope dims. Spousal abuse needs to be stopped for the abused, the abuser, and especially for the children. Allowing children to witness cruel behavior is wrong. The time to hold an abuser accountable is not after the damage has been done to the next generation.

Not all troubles in marriage are equally caused by both partners. Joseph Fielding Smith said: "If a man or a woman who has been sealed in the temple for time and eternity should sin and lose the right to receive the exaltation in the celestial kingdom, he or she could not retard the progress of the injured companion who had been faithful. Everyone will be judged according to his [own] works, and there would be no justice in condemning the innocent for the sins of the guilty."[1]

SUPPORTING THOSE WHO LEAVE ABUSIVE MARRIAGES

Those who choose to leave an abusive marriage are often faced with negative reactions from those around them. When someone has the courage to hold her abuser accountable for his actions, too often others make the situation even more difficult with ill-informed comments. Some tell victims to be more forgiving or to love their spouses more fully. Others tell the victim that God is testing her or that she should change her attitude. Denying the seriousness of abuse is not helpful. Judging divorced individuals or assuming they are guilty can make a very difficult situation even worse. Those who divorce should not be considered less forgiving than those who choose to stay in abusive marital relationships.

When someone takes a stand and leaves a destructive relationship, she needs information, support, and friendship. It takes courage to protect yourself and your children from further abuse, particularly when your greatest goal in life has always been an eternal marriage. Betrayal by others who don't understand can make the choice to separate or divorce as difficult as living in an abusive marriage. Those who have never divorced should realize faithful men and women who leave their marriages first give careful and heart-wrenching thought and prayer to their situation, asking themselves these hard questions:

- How much suffering is required before the continuation of my marriage is a greater evil than divorce?
- What is my moral obligation to my spouse, who denies any responsibility for ongoing abuse and refuses to participate in family therapy or to change his behavior?
- How long is it safe for me and my children to wait and hope for change?
- Will the hope that things will improve some day justify the risk I take of exposing myself and my children to further abuse?"

UNDERSTANDING HEALTHY FAMILY RELATIONSHIP PATTERNS

Most abusers grew up in an abusive family and don't realize their present behavior is wrong. They have learned ways to interact in close relationships that are manipulative, dangerous, controlling, and painful. Many abusers are actually reliving their past unresolved issues in their present relationships. When abused and neglected children become adults and marry, their spouses and children are forced to deal with the consequences. An abuser must face the truth about his past and feel the pain, and then see his cruel behavior as wrong before any lasting change can be made. Most abusers cling to the unhealthy relationship patterns they know like a drowning man dragging his rescuer down with him. They do not understand that healthy relationships

- are calm, not frantic.
- feel relaxed, not forced.
- are accepting of the need for privacy.
- are respectful of differences and opinions.
- are uplifting to both people.
- exhibit an equal sharing of power and control.
- set no unrealistic demands or expectations.
- require each person to accept responsibility for his or her own feelings and behavior.

- allow both people to share in the decision-making process.
- give each person freedom to express all emotions.
- involve people who are committed to communicate effectively.

WE OFTEN REPEAT WHAT WE CAN'T FORGIVE

One man told me about his personal awakening that helped turn his life around. He was a Church leader, successful businessman, and well-respected citizen in the community. He never entertained the idea that he might be neglecting his family. This man said he'd grown up with a violent, alcoholic father who abandoned his family, leaving his mother to live in poverty. This man hated his father and determined that when he married and had a family he would be nothing like his father. After he and his wife had been married for twenty years, she asked for a divorce. His two teenage sons were also having problems with drug addiction at the time. In that time of crisis, he was forced to look at himself for answers. That's when he realized his whole life had been a bitter reaction to his father's choices. He'd become a workaholic, taking great pride in his large home and expensive cars because they proved he was better than his father. He thought his positions in the Church were proof of his righteousness. After his wife left him and he attended counseling sessions with his sons, this man developed a new perspective. He realized that what his family needed most was not the big house, expensive cars, or the father who sat on the stand at church. What they needed was his undivided time, attention, and love.

That's when he realized he'd repeated his father's legacy. He'd just replaced his father's addiction to alcohol with an addiction to acquiring wealth and prestige. Though he'd never physically abandoned his wife and children, he had emotionally abandoned them, forcing them to live in the loveless poverty of an absent and uncommunicative husband and father. Now he was watching his own sons repeat the family legacy with yet another addiction.

> I was so afraid my wife would leave me like my father did. So I kept my distance from her, never getting too close so I couldn't be hurt like that again. I didn't hit her or scream at her, but I didn't talk to her either. I didn't spend time with her. My counselor says I don't know how to love. That's all I want to do now; learn how to love.

Though he did not know it at this time of despair, this man was opening the door of hope for his family. By acknowledging his mistakes and taking steps to change and forgive both himself and his father, he was allowing the Atonement to help him heal. When one member of a family heals, it offers hope to all family members, both living and dead. How we deal with unrequited love will determine the quality of our lives.

REAL LOVE DOESN'T HURT

Those who have been abused need to be told that real love doesn't hurt. "There is no fear in love; but perfect love casteth out fear" (1 John 4:1). When one spouse chooses to see the painful reality of their abusive marriage relationship and then also chooses to leave that reality behind for something better, healing can come to generations past, present, and future. We are all accountable for our choices. "Husband and wife have a solemn responsibility to love and care for each other and for their children. . . . Husbands and wives—mothers and fathers—will be held accountable before God for the discharge of these obligations."[2]

Some fear losing their sealing blessings when their partner in a temple marriage breaks her covenants. We all are individually accountable for our covenants with God. No promised blessing will be denied a covenant-keeping spouse. A covenant is an agreement between us and God. Each individual in a marriage covenant has the sole responsibility to keep his or her promise. The sealing ordinance has no power to bind a husband and wife when one spouse has chosen to break their marriage vows and no power to bind a husband and wife who no longer love each other.

Marriage can be the ultimate refining process. This refining process does not include tolerating abuse. If those in the marriage relationship are faithful, unselfish, and loving, both spouses have the continual opportunity to grow and develop. If those in the marriage relationship are abusive, unfaithful, and selfish, both spouses are held back in their ability to grow and develop as sons and daughters of God. We can rest assured that no blessing will be denied anyone who is faithful and endures to the end. God has promised all losses will be made up to us in the resurrection if we are faithful. Whether in this life or the next, each person who keeps God's commandments and who honors his or her covenants will be granted the blessing of being sealed to a loving eternal companion.

NOTES

1. *Doctrines of Salvation*, 3 vols., comp. Bruce R. McConkie (Salt Lake City: Deseret Book, 1954–56), 2:177.
2. "The Family: A Proclamation to the World," *Ensign*, Nov. 1995, 102.

Chapter Eleven

A Better Way for Families

Family members who abuse other family members create a minia-
ture sick society. When abuse is tolerated, everyone in the family
is harmed and the damage goes on and on for generations. When
victims choose to end destructive relationships and make a conscious
choice to create a better life than the one they've known, the destructive effects of abuse do not have to continue into the next generation. There is hope and healing available for everyone if victims face
reality, mourn what might have been, and then choose to heal and
provide for someone else what they were denied. A woman described
the moment when she decided her abusive past would not be her
present or future this way:

> One day I was in the doctor's office waiting for my appointment.
> A mother and daughter came into the waiting room, sat next to each
> other and starting talking. I could literally feel their mutual love and
> friendship. They had everything I longed for and didn't have. I was
> so overcome, I ran from the waiting room and climbed inside my car
> so I could be alone. I didn't want to embarrass myself by making an
> emotional display in public. Then I sobbed so loud I scared myself. I
> finally accepted I would never have a relationship like that with my
> mother. I had to mourn. After I had a good cry, I placed my hands
> gently on my tummy bulging with my unborn daughter. I asked
> God to help me become the loving mother this child deserved. I was
> determined to provide for her all the love, support, peace, safety, and
> security I never experienced. Now, my daughter is grown and by
> the grace of God we have the loving mother-daughter relationship I
> observed years ago.

Changing unhealthy family relationship patterns takes courage and determination. We have the opportunity to change unhealthy family patterns if we:

- Recognize that the way we think, feel, and behave is stuck.
- Accept that we have a broken reality developed from abuse.
- Mourn for the healthy, loving family situation we didn't have.
- Commit to change what we have known for something better.
- Invite the gifts of the Atonement into our lives.
- Focus on the present and become a Christlike person.

ACCEPTING PAINFUL TRUTHS AND MOVING ON

It is difficult to accept the truth that our family members did not concern themselves with our welfare. They did what they did to make their life easier for them. Because most who abuse never own up to their mistakes or continue to make excuses, there is no forward progress until victims accept reality and choose a better way. When family members are dangerous or destructive, their presence should be minimized, controlled, or eliminated.

Many of us live our lives in an unconscious response to our childhood. Whether the abuse we experienced was physical, emotional, verbal, sexual, or spiritual, each act seared into our souls the great lie that we are unlovable, unworthy, not good enough, unworthy of respect, less than others, and of no consequence. Over time, these lies cloud our thinking until we no longer see the truth. The way we feel about ourselves and others is viewed in the context of this huge distortion. The truth is that each of us is a priceless soul with unlimited potential.

Most people who refuse to acknowledge that abuse occurred in their homes become remarkably similar to the abuser. Our mother and father gave us life and the opportunity to experience mortality. For that alone they deserve our gratitude. That gratitude must not cloud our ability to see the truth. As we acknowledge any abuse and understand the effect that abuse had on us, we allow ourselves to feel pain and loss so that we will not want to pass it on.

Contrary to what some family members will tell us, our refusal to deny, tolerate, or hide abuse is an act of integrity, not betrayal. When we attempt to keep ourselves safe from further abuse, some family members may blame, accuse, or threaten. We can experience inner peace even if others choose to continue living lives of contention, confrontation, and chaos. Only our Father in Heaven can bless us with personal peace and an accurate view of our identity and worth. When we're filled with God's love, we don't concern ourselves with how we appear to others. We're able to stand alone.

If we were abused as a child, we did not have the mental ability to discern an abusive parent; we saw only an inadequate self. We learned we had no value and could not trust people. We didn't learn to bond in healthy ways. We may have become overly perfectionistic in an unconscious attempt to prove that what our abuser said is not true. We are often mean to ourselves because it feels normal. We carry a nagging sense of personal failure. We believe the horrible things we were told and try to hide constant self-doubt that tells us we are unworthy or unlovable. All these reactions to childhood abuse can be overcome. We can't control the purity of the water upstream from us, but with God's help we can control the purity of the water we send downstream.

Everyone has several chances to have a happy childhood. The first time is when we're growing up. The second time is when we have the opportunity to re-experience or reexamine the idea of childhood with our own children while they are growing up or by associating with other children. For late bloomers, there are third and fourth chances with grandchildren and great-grandchildren. Jesus lovingly told us how to become as a child and go to him for healing when he offered this counsel: "Verily I say unto you, Except ye be converted, and become as little children, ye shall not enter into the kingdom of heaven. Whosoever therefore shall humble himself as this little child, the same is greatest in the kingdom of heaven. And whoso shall receive one such little child in my name receiveth me." (Matthew 18:3–5). The Savior can and will heal us if we are converted and act on his promise by becoming "submissive, meek, humble, patient, full of love" (Mosiah 3:19).

LEAVING HOME

We all had to leave our heavenly home to discover important truths about ourselves in mortality through the use of agency. One of the reasons we left premortal life was to learn to discern good from evil. We are constantly pulled and required to choose between the two. We are also asked to leave our mortal parents to learn to discern between the good and evil we experienced there. "Therefore shall a man leave his father and his mother, and shall cleave unto his wife: and they shall be one flesh" (Genesis 2:24). When we leave our parents' home, we are given a new chance to evaluate what took place there. We must decide what patterns of behavior to take with us and what to leave behind as we create a new family.

Many who were abused as children have an unhealthy attachment to their parents and extended family members. They have a difficult time developing their independence and setting healthy boundaries without overwhelming feelings of fear, doubt, and guilt. Though it is difficult, abuse survivors must accept the fact that their relationships with abusive family members will never get better if they continue to tolerate cruel behavior. Destructive relationships entangle both abusers and victims in a web of deception and fear.

No one can satisfy our longing for what we never received as a child from our parents or siblings, not even our parents or siblings now. To involve others in this hopeless search is to lose opportunities before us today. The opportunity before us today is to provide for someone else the love we were denied. All hope lies in the present. Love begets love.

Leaving home means leaving behind unloving relationships with family members and moving forward with complete trust in God. We can choose something better. We may need distance, separation, and counseling so we can evaluate the effect toxic family relationships have had on us. It takes courage to swim against the family tide and insist on healthy relationships and boundaries. We have the right to a peaceful life and must give highest priority to our personal safety and sanity. Elder Russell M. Nelson taught, "Because the work (and glory) of God is to bring to pass our immortality and eternal life as a family, it logically follows that the work of the adversary will strike directly at the heart of the home—the family"[1]

CREATING A LOVING ENVIRONMENT

We can create a healthy loving environment for ourselves and our children as we do the following things:

Practice loving communication. Too many homes have too many love-starved people; we need to feed them. Compliments and expressions of appreciation are like food for a starving soul. All of us need the feeling of being appreciated, valued, and recognized.

Lay down weapons of war. Book of Mormon stories offer examples of how behavior changes when hearts change. "And as many as were convinced did lay down their weapons of war, and also their hatred and the tradition of their fathers" (Helaman 5:51). When abuse is going on in the family and we tolerate it, the whole family is at war. Everyone loses in a family war.

Choose Christ as our partner. Every abuse victim is entitled to peace in this life. A just God has provided a way for the innocent to find peace through the Atonement. Christ can and will carry the burdens of the innocent. We are never alone. "I will go before your face. I will be on your right hand and on your left, and my Spirit shall be in your hearts, and mine angels round about you, to bear you up" (D&C 84:88).

Let go of fear. We can create a better life than we have known. "Fear not: for they that be with us are more than they that be with them" (2 Kings 6:16). Jesus took upon himself every abuse and knows how to comfort us. We are each invited to come to Christ with every burden, scar, terror, and fear—and find rest.

Receive compensating blessings. Justice demands compensating blessings for every particle of suffering we experience, through no fault of our own, in this life. God provided us with a Savior who can fill our empty souls with joy, light, and sweetness. We don't need to concern ourselves that some abusers will die without ever feeling any guilt, confessing, or being punished. Some abusers will have sterling reputations, wealth, good health, and glowing funerals. We can rest assured that the demands of justice go beyond the veil.

Forgive. By leaving ultimate judgment to our Creator, we can have peace in this life. When we forgive before our offender repents, we place ourselves in God's loving care and our hearts become open to receive more peace, comfort, and direction. Every challenge we face presents us with a choice. Pain allows our souls to develop traits of tenderness, kindness, and understanding. Job and Joseph Smith provide us with examples of those who endured well.

Look for pain we may have caused. I often hear the remark, "Well, my parents did it to me and I turned out all right." I answer, maybe you didn't. Perhaps you have been scarred in ways you don't realize. Maybe you justify your parents' behavior as a way to stay numb to the pain you have caused your own spouse and children. For example, even if you don't repeat the legacy of sexual abuse you experienced, perhaps you have been unable to give your family members normal, healthy physical affection. For another example, even if you don't repeat the legacy of physical abuse you experienced as a child, you may be distant, detached, and lack an innate ability to play or express your love. Even if you don't repeat the verbal and emotional abuse you experienced as a child, you may lack feelings of self-worth and be racked with fears you unknowingly pass down to the next generation. And lastly, even if you don't repeat the spiritual abuse you experienced as a child, you may deny your child spiritual opportunities by staying away from anything related to religion.

SAVING THE NEXT GENERATION

Those who don't understand the damage done to innocent, developing spirits by abuse believe victims should simply get on with their lives. Those who have had a life filled with pain, fear, threats, and feelings of guilt, unworthiness, and sadness need a safe place and time to heal. For those who suffered sexual abuse, the beauty of their sexuality has been compromised. For those who suffered physical abuse, the safety of their world has been compromised. For those who suffered emotional abuse, the awareness of their own divine worth has been compromised. For those who suffered spiritual abuse, religious observance brings feelings of guilt, fear, and self-doubt.

One of the surest ways to heal is to provide for someone else what was denied to us or to focus on saving the next generation. Parents can learn new respect for their own innocence as they experience the innocence of their child. "They must . . . humble themselves as their

115

little children, and they shall all be saved with their little children" (Moroni 8:10). Parents can learn patience for their inadequacies as they experience patience for their child. Parents can learn about their own priceless individuality as they treasure the uniqueness of their child. Parents can heal from feelings of abandonment by providing safety and stability for their children. Parents can be healed of trust issues as they become a person their children can trust. Parents can be healed of fear as they guide their children into life and re-explore the world as a friendly and happy place. By becoming the loving parents each child needs, we heal.

We must cut out the cancer of abuse before it moves to the next generation. We must end relationships that are compromising our mental, spiritual, and physical health. We must not allow dangerous and destructive people access to us or our children. It is self-deception when we keep holding on and doing what ever it takes to have a relationship with a family member because we think this will eventually bring us peace. In fact, acceptance of reality is the only true way to peace.

We've been promised by prophets that if we build our families on the rock of our Savior, our homes will become sanctuaries where family members will be sheltered from the dark and raging storms around us. The Savior's infinite Atonement, coupled with sacred covenants, makes it possible for us to dwell with our families forever. Families who receive the gifts of the Atonement of Jesus Christ are built on the rock that will not fall. A rich, rewarding, and abundant life is possible for all of us. "I am come that they might have life, and that they might have it more abundantly" (John 10:10). Raising a new generation of innocent children with Christlike love can literally change the world.

NOTE

1.   Russell M. Nelson, "Set in Order Thy House," *Ensign*, Nov. 2001, 71.

Chapter Twelve

THE POWER OF PRAYER

Personal conversations with our Heavenly Father can enlist the powers of heaven in our behalf. We need the armor of heaven to face the battles of life. God always hears and answers prayers. Though at times it seems our supplications to God are not answered, they are. Prayers offered in faith are always answered, though not always in the manner or the time frame we desire. God doesn't give us everything we want, but everything we need. All humble, sincere prayers are recorded in heaven and will eventually bear fruit.

I once spoke with a woman who was still reeling from the murder of her son. "I've prayed every day of my life for God to protect my children from harm and danger. Then something like this happens. Why? Why should I even bother praying? What good is praying anyway? What difference does it make? It doesn't change anything."

Her questions deserve thoughtful examination. Why should we bother praying if it doesn't change anything? We pray because praying changes us. God doesn't need changing.

One woman described the eventual effect of her simple prayers as an abused child this way:

> I used to pray and ask God to make my mom stop hurting me. She kept hurting me. I used to pray and ask God to make my dad help me. He didn't. Then I decided to try a different tactic. I asked God to make me fast so I could outrun my mother. Sometimes I was fast enough, and sometimes she caught me.
>
> I eventually discovered that though God didn't work a miracle for me in those dark days in my childhood, in time He worked a miracle in me. Who would ever suppose that terrified little girl would

one day be surrounded by a husband, children, and grandchildren to love and be loved by? Who I am today is an answered prayer—and my own personal miracle. God couldn't force my parents to love me, but He kept love alive deep inside of me.

Most of us pray like children insisting that God intervene in our behalf by taking away the agency of others. We ask our Creator to force other people to behave the way we want them to and then feel sad, mad, or betrayed when we don't get our prayers answered according to our demands. Sometimes our supplications sound as though we've forgotten about our personal agreement to the terms of mortality.

THE BEGINNING OF REVERENCE

When we pray, we allow ourselves to have an experience with someone beyond what we can see, touch, and hear. Prayer is our connection to something greater than ourselves; it is our personal, sacred union with the divine. We all have access to God twenty-four hours a day; He is always there, always listens, and always seeks to bless us.

One woman described how her experience with prayer helped her survive an abusive childhood this way:

> While I was growing up I often went to secret places in our yard where I could hide and pray for help. I remember one particular day when I ran to my hiding place after a beating. Every cell in my body ached to be comforted but there was no one in my life to care. I remember lying face down on the ground clawing at the dirt, trying desperately to be held. I wept with such intensity that my tears soon turned the dirt near my face into pools of mud.
>
> "Heavenly Father," I plead, "please hold me."
>
> I felt the damp warmth of the earth soak into my skin and instinctively knew I was loved. I rolled over and saw light filtering through the leaves above me, creating a moving display of both shimmering iridescence and shadow. I felt the presence of a power that calmed and reassured me. I felt small, yet not diminished. I sat up and felt the wind on my cheek like a gentle caress. I believe now that what I was feeling was reverence and divine love, even though I didn't give it a name. I longed to draw closer, as if I were filled with liquid sunshine. I felt as though I were near another place of ultimate beauty and love, as if the flutter of the next breeze would part the veil

and I could momentarily catch a glimpse of a world far better than the one I knew.

I often felt beautiful things about myself and others during these prayerful times. Once, I saw tiny, brilliant lights circling around my head. I remember counting them one by one. Just for an instant the lights became faces, bright smiling faces all around me and through me, filling me with comfort and joy. At the time, I fancied these faces were my guardian angels. I've since wondered if these faces of light were my children, yet unborn.

Other times I felt loving words fill my mind, such as, "I love you. Don't be scared. You're not alone. I'm with you." What I felt was in such stark contrast to what I heard in my home, I was profoundly amazed. During these prayerful times, I sensed invisible assistance surrounding me with safety. Because of these deeply spiritual times, I had no trouble believing Joseph Smith had seen God and Jesus Christ as the result of a simple prayer. I knew God spoke to fourteen-year-old boys and to frightened little girls.

While I was praying, I knew God had things for me to do and a purpose I did not yet understand. I went away from these prayerful times with a tiny glimpse of another reality. My home felt like old black-and-white horror movies—fake, false, and frightening. The world I felt as I prayed was a full-color, first-run movie spectacular—exciting, joyful, and real. I was experiencing a loving relationship with God through prayer. The love I experienced when I prayed as a child gave me something to hope for when I later married and created a home of my own. I wanted a home that felt like I felt when I prayed.

LIFE PRAYER

Prayer can be thought of as a carefully designed pattern of living. The elements of life prayer can be combined or experienced in any order that suits your needs throughout the day. The important thing is actually making a real connection with God. Each person can develop his or her own daily meditative routine for optimal well-being. The following might be helpful:

Solitude. Find a place to be physically alone. If not possible, imagine you are alone.

Movement. Go for a walk or exercise in your home. Move until you break a sweat and the achy, tight, heavy, or sluggish feeling in your mind and body lifts.

Nature. Surround yourself with nature, either real or imagined. You can do this by lying on the grass in the backyard or sitting on a chair in your bedroom and imagining you're in your favorite place outdoors.

Body awareness. Starting at your toes and working upward and out the top of your head become aware of every part of your body. Notice where you feel tight or anxious, and imagine that your body suddenly melts and becomes like sand flowing out from you. If you have a hard time relaxing, first tighten the muscles in the area of your body that is tense and then slowly relax so you can feel the contrast.

Surroundings awareness. This should be done after you are relaxed and feel a connection between your body and spirit. If you're outside, allow yourself to feel the wind blowing your hair or feel warm sun on your face. Listen to the sound of birds. In your home, smell breakfast cooking in the kitchen or listen to the laughter of your children in the other room. Surroundings awareness can be either real or imagined. If your surroundings are not all you would hope for, imagine something more or different.

Music. Listen to or perform music that lifts and renews.

Imagination. Take a journey in your imagination. Imagine you are with your Heavenly Parents. Feel their arms surround you. Imagine you are kneeling at the feet of Jesus, giving him your deepest sadness. Imagine you are doing something positive you've always wanted to do.

Stillness. Enter into stillness. Allow your mind to empty of all thoughts for a moment, and let peace and safety enter every cell of your body.

Pray. Kneel, if possible. Make your prayers vocal if possible. Address your Father in Heaven. Express your heartfelt appreciation. Talk to God about everything you are concerned about. Ask for guidance and direction. Give your will to God and ask what you should do today that matters most. Close your conversation in the name of Jesus Christ.

Listen. Be still and listen. Listening is the most important part of praying. Don't just listen with your ears—hear with your heart.

Read. Read something edifying that enlarges your knowledge and understanding beyond your limited life experiences. Read the scriptures and other good books.

Create. Create something based on your experience with prayer. This is one way for your imagination to become real. The process of creating something from your hopes makes wishing grow into faith, then faith grow into action, and action grow into reality.

All these components of life prayer work together to create an existence that is both simple and sacred. Solitude, movement, nature, body and surroundings awareness, music, imagination, stillness, prayer, and listening can be accomplished by simply going for a walk in nature first thing in the morning. Music, reading, and creating can be accomplished by performing or listening to uplifting music before reading your scriptures and writing in your journal. All these elements of life prayer make for a meaningful life—not a life without problems, but a life fully lived in the midst of both pain and joy. When your day is scheduled to include life prayer, you will feel peace and experience life with deeper awareness. Nothing life throws at you during the day can disrupt the closeness you feel to God. No lie you hear about yourself or others can deceive you about the sacredness of human potential. Your mind, body, and spirit become a conduit for the Holy Ghost.

WHAT DO WE PRAY FOR?

Here are some blessings we can pray for if we desire to heal from abuse:

- To feel God's love
- To know God and Jesus Christ
- To have knowledge and peace about our standing before God
- To lay our burden at the feet of the Savior
- To receive new information and insight on what actions to take to help us heal
- To be directed to a qualified professional
- To have faith in our future
- To let go of our past
- For the resources and skills we need to help us heal
- For courage to remove abusive people from our life

- For supportive friends and Church members
- For strength to overcome adversity
- For help seeing ourselves as God sees us
- For help seeing others as God sees them
- For help to repent and forgive both ourselves and others

Prayers of faith are always answered. We are known and loved by our Creator, who has perfect knowledge of what is best for us. When we pray to know God's will and then submit with patience and courage to what happens to us in this life, we will be guided and healed in God's time and God's way. There is a direct relationship between how we feel about ourselves and others and how close we are to God. The way we view ourselves, the clear picture we have of who we were, are, and can become comes into sharp focus when we have a present, ongoing, and loving relationship with our Creator. Without that divine, nourishing relationship, we depend on outside influences and mortal relationships that often give us a distorted self-image or a limited view of our true nature and eternal potential. Those who are abused in childhood often have a mental image of self and others that is false, a lie.

If we ask in faith with a broken heart and contrite spirit, God will help us see the truth about ourselves and those around us. If we ask in faith, we will feel God's love for us and see ourselves as we really are. When we personally feel God's love for us, our problems and challenges become pathways for growth and development. God always hears and answers our prayers.

WHY DO WE NEED TO PRAY?

Honest, heartfelt prayer invites God to speak directly to us. Prayer helps us to see our weaknesses and strengths. Prayer opens our minds and hearts to a different way of viewing the same old situations and relationship challenges. Without the Atonement, those of us who were raised in loveless homes would be left on our own, dominated by heredity, upbringing, and natural desires. We wouldn't know how to love, because we would not have yet experienced love. Through prayer, we can turn to God when we are lonely, in pain, afraid, terrified, betrayed, let down, or disappointed. Because of prayer, we can take our broken heart to God, seeking His assistance, and take our love to our family. When we acknowledge our need for help, we invite divine direction, personal insights, and spiritual strength. Answers to prayer always will come in God's time and in God's way.

THE PARABLE OF SEVEN

God reassures us that we don't need to be afraid. "Fear not," we hear in the scriptures. Yet life keeps coming at us with one problem, dilemma, or trauma after another. Before we're finished reeling from one challenge, we're confronted with another. We end up feeling chronically overwhelmed and underqualified to handle our own life and complex relationships.

I remember playing piano in Church meetings as a teenager. The chorister expected me to play the hymns flawlessly without giving me the pieces to practice before church began. I wasn't an accomplished pianist and had a difficult time playing anything written in more than three sharps or four flats. In essence, I was always scared and never performed well. Forty years later, someone mentioned that a pianist can change the sharps to flats or the flats to sharps in any piece of music as long as it added up to seven. So if the music is written in five sharps, you can play it with two flats. Or if the music is written in six flats, you can play it in one sharp. I was elated. I'd spent a lifetime trying to sight-read music in church and feeling stressed and embarrassed when the piece was written with too many sharps or flats. I had no idea you could do it any other way. That was all I knew.

Similarly, most of us struggle through life with a very limited view of the multitude of possibilities open to us. We know what we know from our background, genetics, and upbringing. Unless we seek answers through prayer and experiment on the words of Christ, we will remain victims simply because we failed to search hard enough for divine solutions to our problems. Because I'd never taken the time to ask for added knowledge from a master teacher or learned the solution to my problem by studying music theory, I struggled with sight-reading phobia for years.

One piece of information, knowledge, or insight can change our life and our perspective forever. God has many personal revelations waiting for us, if we want to know, ask, and listen, and if we are willing to act on our new knowledge. Prayer is not mortal us telling our omnipotent God what to do, nor is it our personal directions to God about how our life should play out. Prayer is the way to gain new insight into our circumstances and the way we begin positive change in ourselves.

We can pray to ask if something is right. "Behold, you have not understood; you have supposed that I would give it unto you, when you took no thought save it was to ask me. But, behold, I say unto you, that you must study it out in your mind; then you must ask me if it be right, and if it is right I will cause that your bosom shall burn within you; therefore, you shall feel that it is right. But if it be not right you shall have no such feelings, but you shall have a stupor of thought" (D&C 9:7–9).

We can pray to have a believing attitude or a forgiving heart. "Therefore I say unto you, what things soever ye desire, when ye pray, believe that ye receive them, and ye shall have them. And when ye stand praying, forgive, if ye have ought against any: that your Father also which is in heaven may forgive you your trespasses" (Mark 11:24–25).

We can pray to remember the greatness of God. "I would that ye should remember, and always retain in remembrance, the greatness of God, and your own nothingness, and his goodness and long-suffering towards you, unworthy creatures, and humble yourselves even in the depths of humility, calling on the name of the Lord daily" (Mosiah 4:11).

We can pray to be filled with the love of Christ. "Pray unto the Father with all the energy of heart, that ye may be filled with this love, which he hath bestowed upon all who are true followers of his Son, Jesus Christ; that ye may become the sons of God; that when he shall appear we shall be like him" (Moroni 7:48).

We can pray for love for those who have abused us. "Behold I say unto you, love your enemies, bless them that curse you, do good to them that hate you, and pray for them who despitefully use you and persecute you; that ye may be the children of your Father who is in heaven; for he maketh his sun to rise on the evil and on the good" (3 Nephi 12:44–45).

We can pray for forgiveness of sins and to know our standing before God. "I betook myself to prayer and supplication to Almighty God for forgiveness of all my sins and follies, and also for a manifestation to me, that I might know of my state and standing before him; for I had full confidence in obtaining a divine manifestation, as I previously had one" (Joseph Smith—History 1:29).

We can pray to have greater understanding and knowledge. "And if thou wilt inquire, thou shalt know mysteries which are great and marvelous; therefore thou shalt exercise thy gift, that thou mayest find out mysteries, that thou mayest bring many to the knowledge of the truth, yea, convince them of the error of their ways" (D&C 6:11).

We can pray to overcome discouragement and depression. "If the Lord in his condescension unto the children of men hath visited men in so much mercy, why should my heart weep and my soul linger in the valley of sorrow. . . . Rejoice, O my heart, and cry unto the Lord, and say: O Lord, I will praise thee forever; yea, my soul will rejoice in thee, my God, and the rock of my salvation. O Lord, wilt thou redeem my soul? Wilt thou deliver me out of the hands of mine enemies? Wilt thou make me that I may shake at the appearance of sin? . . . O Lord, wilt thou encircle me around in the robe of thy righteousness! O Lord, wilt thou make a way for mine escape before mine enemies! Wilt thou make my path straight before me! . . . O Lord, I have trusted in thee, and I will trust in thee forever. . . . I will cry unto thee, my God, the rock of my righteousness. Behold, my voice shall forever ascend up unto thee, my rock and mine everlasting God" (2 Nephi 4:26, 30–31, 33–35; see verses 15–35).

UNEXPECTED ANSWERS TO PRAYER

Answers to prayer often come in unexpected packages—but they always come. Some answers come as moments of unexpected light and joy. For example, early in her pregnancy my daughter had an ultrasound that revealed her unborn child would have many physical challenges. We all prayed in faith that this child would be made "well and whole." Our prayers were heard and answered, only not quite the way we expected. When this child was born, he was missing his brain and one of his eyes. The doctors said he would die soon after birth because his body was "not compatible with life." All professionals agreed he would exist in a chronic vegetative state and would have no quality of life. Those who love this child soon discovered experts don't always have all the answers. We've learned something about the dignity of the immortal soul and possess a deeper knowledge about what it means to be "well and whole." Through him, we've learned that the resiliency of the human spirit is powerful, eternal, and sacred. This child, even with grave physical limitations, still proved to be capable of growth in spite of the immense challenges. You would be moved if you witnessed his efforts to develop with the limitations of his mortal body. Your heart would be forever changed if you watched his family assist him.

The doctors say Caleb cannot see, hear, feel, taste, touch, think, or even move on his own. They say he has no consciousness and any movement is only a reflex. What the doctors don't understand is that this child has an immortal spirit residing inside his mortal body that communicates he is happy to be here, grateful for his body, joyful to have a loving family, and thankful for all efforts to help him. This child's single eye has given several scriptures new meaning. "And if your eye be single to my glory, your whole bodies shall be filled with light, and there shall be no darkness in you; and that body which is filled with light comprehendeth all things" (D&C 88:67). This child is filled with light. His family is convinced his only eye is truly "single" to the glory of God, for when others in the neighborhood are having a hard time, they ask if they can come over to the house and hold him. He comforts their broken hearts and helps them see others through the eyes of love.

Before he was born, our family had a secret code to communicate love for each other when we are out in public. We wink. When one of us is about to perform or speak, we find a family member's face in the crowd. That family member will quickly wink at us. Winking is our secret code for saying, "I love you. You can do it. You're wonderful." This child knew he would never be able to speak a word in mortality—so he found a way. When he was born with one eyelid permanently winking, the whole family took it as a sign from an eternal family member who knows and loves us. This child is always winking, always saying, "I love you. You can do it. You're wonderful."

Caleb shines. Our family is ministered to by the light of his spirit. The medical community sees his limitations; we see his strengths. The experts see his missing parts and predict a dismal prognosis; we experience joy in his presence today. Because of him, we understand we can never take a day on earth for granted. Our sadness, anxiety, and fear of losing this precious child at any moment has been transformed into joy. "Thou hast turned . . . my mourning into dancing: thou hast put off my sackcloth, and girded me with gladness; to the end that my glory may sing praise to thee, and not be silent. O Lord my God, I will give thanks unto thee forever" (Psalm 30:11–12).

Caleb lived for seven years. Taking care of him was a sacred, joyful, and holy experience for every member of his family. Caleb's life was not about what we did for him; it was about what Caleb did for us.

No matter what challenges we face in mortality, God truly can change our deepest fears and sorrows into joy. Through the love of God and Christ's Atonement, we will all be "well and whole." There is always hope where there is love—and where there is love, there are miracles. I know miracles happen around us every day. Love is the greatest power in the universe. If we are patient and trust God, spring will come, the sun will rise after the darkest night, and love will return where only hurt and pain now reside. That is God's promise.

A LINK TO THE DIVINE

Prayer is the most underrated gift we have in mortality. At any moment, at any place, we can direct our thoughts to heaven through the name of our Savior Jesus Christ and effectively call home. We are all alike to God and equally loved. "There has come to you as your birthright something beautiful and sacred and divine. Never forget that. Your Eternal Father is the great Master of the universe. He rules over all, but He also will listen to your prayers . . . and hear you as you speak with Him. He will answer your prayers. He will not leave you alone."[1]

Though sometimes it feels otherwise, we are never alone. We do not have to make it on our own. "Never assume that you can make it alone. You need the help of the Lord. Never hesitate to get on your knees in some private place and speak with Him. What a marvelous and wonderful thing is prayer. Think of it. We can actually speak with our Father in Heaven. He will hear and respond, but we need to listen to that response. Nothing is too serious and nothing too unimportant to share with Him."[2] With prayer as our precious channel of communication with God, we need never feel alone or comfortless again.

NOTES

1. Gordon B. Hinckley, "Stay on the High Road," *Ensign*, May 2004, 112.
2. Ibid., 114.

Section Four

HOW TO HEAL
AND MOVE FORWARD

Chapter Thirteen

WHY FORGIVENESS?

My friend is a banker. Once we were discussing his profession's practice of writing off bad loans—the money a customer has borrowed and never paid back. Even after the process of bankruptcy and foreclosure, his bank is often left holding the bag while the debtor seems to get off free. When he told me about several large loans his bank had made in the past that were never repaid and the resulting branch office closures and employee layoffs, I wondered if the erring borrowers fully understood the results of their unwillingness or inability to repay their loans.

"Doesn't every debtor have the moral responsibility to repay every loan no matter how long it takes?" I asked.

"After bankruptcy and foreclosure the borrower no longer has the legal responsibility," he answered. "At that point the responsibility is a moral one. What happens next is between the debtor and God. Somewhere along the way, we decide it's in our best interest to write off the loan and get on with business."

This practice seemed unfair because I'd personally known the men and women who had lost their employment as a result of those unpaid debts. I saw firsthand the effect the unpaid loans had on the bankers' families and futures. Those loans were made in good faith with the promise they would be repaid someday. They never were. The passing years have taught me to see justice in a different light.

When someone takes something from us and doesn't give it back or attempt to make restitution, we are given a choice. After legal responsibilities and Church accountability are met, we can spend our lives tending to the unpaid debt, focusing on all the things we'd do if the debt were paid, using the debt as justification for our bitter feelings—or we can write off the loan, absorb the loss, and get on with the business of today. If we forgive the debt, it is so we can free ourselves, not the debtor. We no longer need to fruitlessly attempt to balance the books because we've balanced the benefits of being free from pain and moving forward into healing. We prize our personal peace of mind and productivity more than our position of moral auditor as we choose to willingly leave the final accounting to God.

When we forgive the debt, we don't send the message to the debtor that he somehow no longer owes the money. He still does. We just don't have to waste any more time being the bill collector. We free ourselves from the burden of keeping track of what the debtor does or doesn't do. We no longer give the debtor power to invade our thoughts and behavior. We are free to live our lives without the chains of fear, resentment, bitterness, and hatred. For many victims, numerous debts will remain unpaid by the debtor in this life. Yet we can be at peace, knowing God is both merciful and just. In the end there are no sins beyond forgiveness, no debts the Atonement cannot satisfy (with the single exception of the unforgivable sin against the Holy Ghost). Only God can balance all accounts.

MISCONCEPTIONS ABOUT FORGIVENESS

Forgiveness is often misunderstood by victims of abuse. Forgiveness doesn't mean we allow ourselves or others to continue to be victimized. It doesn't mean we allow the abuser in our life. On the contrary, understanding the evil of abuse and doing all in our power to stop it must come first. After we've taken the necessary steps to report abuse to civil and Church authorities and other family members for their protection, we can begin a personal journey to healing. Forgiveness is an important step in that journey. Many people would rather die than forgive, and they do—they die in unforgiveness. Ultimately no one "gets away" with anything. We don't have to keep track of whether or not a sinner repents. Everyone will stand before God some day. No one can permanently run away from accountability. Forgiveness is part of a continuing process of releasing ourselves from the negative effects of abuse.

There are several myths about forgiveness. One myth is that we can't forgive because we can't forget. In truth, when we forgive, we are granted the ability to remember in a different way. Another myth is that if we forgive it means we now trust the person who harmed us. Forgiveness doesn't mean we become stupid or naïve. Forgiveness makes us stronger, not weaker, and wiser, not more vulnerable. When we forgive it means we've decided not to invest any more energy into being angry or bitter. Anger may be a necessary part of the grieving process, but we don't have to stay angry to protect ourselves indefinitely. Another popular myth about forgiveness is that some people are so awful they don't deserve to be forgiven. Forgiveness is something we do for ourselves; whether or not the abuser deserves our forgiveness is irrelevant. It is important to remember that we may never know what the abuser suffered as an innocent victim.

Some people are afraid if they forgive, the abuser will do it again. First we should do all in our power to hold the abuser accountable so that we are not willingly abused by that person again. Then, because we do not have total control over others, we need to decide what we are going to do differently in the future to deal with abusive behavior. If we are determined not to forgive until the abuser admits the abuse and asks for forgiveness, we have given ourselves a built-in excuse for staying bitter. This excuse gives the abuser continuing control over us.

> I would like to make it clear that forgiveness of sins should not be confused with tolerating evil. . . . The Savior asks us to forsake and combat evil in all its forms. Although we must forgive a neighbor who injures us we should work constructively to prevent that injury from being repeated. A woman who is abused should not seek revenge, but neither should she feel she cannot take steps to prevent further abuse. Forgiveness does not require us to accept or tolerate evil. It does not require us to ignore the wrong that we see in the world around us or in our own lives.[1]

There is no way to genuinely forgive without experiencing a great deal of personal spiritual growth. When we the forgive, God helps us understand we have no right to do wrong to another human being, even when wrong has been done to us. We can't force ourselves to forgive immediately, but as we live gospel principles we will be ready when forgiveness comes. Forgiveness is a voluntary act that untangles us from the abuser's web and frees us from negative emotions. The Savior tells us to forgive our enemies: "I, the Lord, will forgive whom I will forgive, but of you it is required to forgive all men" (D&C 64:10). If we desire forgiveness from God, we need to work through the process of forgiving those who have harmed us.

Forgiveness enlightens and empowers the injured. When we forgive, we allow God to work a great miracle in us. We access the power of the Atonement and allow our Creator to flood our soul with joy and peace. The light that comes from Jesus Christ is always stronger than even the greatest darkness. All unrepented and unforgiven sins leave a hole in our spirit that allows the powers of darkness to enter. One of the most beautiful stories about forgiveness is that of the prodigal son, found in Luke. In some ways, we are all the prodigal son and his father. We are all in dire need of forgiveness, and we all need to forgive.

Forgiveness may or may not involve a reunion or reconciliation with the person who abused us, but it does always mean a reunion and reconciliation with God and our own peace of mind. Chronic victims are in too much pain to "love [their] enemies, bless them that curse [them], do good to them that hate [them], and pray for them which despitefully use [them], and persecute [them]" (Matthew 5:44). Forgiveness is a step we take when we decide to stop living life as a victim. We choose whether or not we stay in destructive relationships. If we don't call on divine help for enlightenment and healing, we will be miserable for much longer than we need to be. God can help see that the abuse we suffered happened for reasons apart from us. We may never know in this lifetime what those reasons are. The abuser may never admit to the abuse, repent, or ask for forgiveness, yet we can still experience the peace of mind and healing that come after forgiveness if we leave the final accounting to God and move on.

Abusive experiences are awful moments, but those moments aren't our whole life. Life is too short to let the actions of others continue to have power over our happiness today. Forgiveness means we let go of what others do and say because they have no real power to harm us in the present—except for the power we give them. Forgiveness takes into account the knowledge that those who hurt us have a history that contributes to their behavior that is apart from us; it thus is possible to develop empathy for them.

Studies have shown that even when abusers are put in jail or excommunicated, it offers little relief to those who have been abused if the victims haven't yet opened the door of forgiveness by receiving the blessings of the Atonement. Those who are angry, bitter, and full of hate will remain angry, bitter, and full of hate even after civil and Church justice is served. The wounds remain unhealed, the life thwarted, and the individual's progress is measurably slowed. We've been counseled about the folly of believing ourselves to be an accurate judge. If we want forgiveness, we are required to forgive. Because of the Atonement, we can all experience a sacred transformation and claim the fruits of our Savior's victory over sin.

I remember a day when the parents of students in my daughter's ballet class were invited to attend a performance demonstration to see the progress of the dance students. There were obvious differences in the levels of ballet technique competency as the girls followed the teacher's commands and performed a choreographed dance for us. I knew my daughter had struggled with shyness for years, along with learning to cope with legs that were several inches different in length. Taking ballet was her idea. She'd found the courage to take classes as a beginner with other girls who had been taking ballet for ten or more years. Watching her dance that day was amazingly beautiful to me. It didn't matter to me how she compared to the other girls. Even her teacher could not possibly know what she had overcome to get to this personal level of grace. Someone attending that class as an observer could not possibly make a judgment that was accurate about her competency or accomplishments. I realized that only a parent who truly knows and loves his or her child can accurately assess the child's progress. So it is with God. Only our loving Father in Heaven can accurately assess His children's progress. When we change our hearts enough to forgive, we unlock the power of grace. We don't just do this for ourselves and our families but in fact for all those who follow us. We owe our children and grandchildren clean and rich earth in which to grow.

Though we cannot guarantee the weather they will have to endure or what seasons of drought or plenty will be theirs, we can provide them with fertile soil where they can sink their roots down deep in our love. We can help them know the way to replenish their ultimate source of life-giving water at the Savior's feet. "Father, forgive them; for they know not what they do," Jesus cried (Luke 23: 34). Christ continues to act as our advocate with the Father—his Atonement was the ultimate act of forgiveness and love.

CLEANSING THE INNER VESSEL

I once watched a professional potter working at the wheel, throwing pots. I asked him questions about the formation of the outer walls and how he made the beautiful, varied shapes he was forming. He told me he just pays attention to the center and the outside walls take care of themselves. So it is with our lives. If we pay attention to our center and take the time to cleanse our own inner vessels, the outer walls will take care of themselves. No family is ever healed until individual members work on themselves first. If we focus on our core relationships with God, we can become a transitional character in our family.

I once received a nasty insect bite when I was living in primitive conditions and didn't have any antibiotic ointment to apply to the injury. Before long, the site became infected, and then the infection spread to all the other parts of my body. What could have been dealt with quickly, had the necessary medicine been available, soon became a major health crisis. Healing from abuse is like that. Without the application of forgiveness, the injury to our spirit spreads and infects our whole life and the lives of all those around us. Injuries to our soul from another's sins cause great pain. Healing from this pain doesn't occur in a magical, transcendent moment that simply descends on us without effort. In fact, part of that effort involves repentance. Repentance means to change and turn our hearts to God. Personal change gives us a fresh view of others and ourselves. Why would I talk about repentance when so much of the pain we experience in life is caused by someone else? Because only in the process of personal change do we soften our hearts enough to let God's love inside. Those who have been abused often need to repent of failing to nurture and protect themselves and of the long-held untrue personal belief that they are not worthy of love and respect. When we repent of this self-betrayal, we open our souls to feel God's infinite and unconditional love.

For example, one woman told me that when she was in her thirties, she went to the hospital for a simple surgery. The doctor cut a nerve accidentally and paralyzed her from the waist down. Then her husband left, leaving her to raise four children from a wheelchair. She shared with me that she tried to sue the doctor, but his friends lied for him. She was bitter at her husband for leaving. She had been wronged. She was suffering through no fault of her own.

Then one day she looked into the eyes of one of her children and felt her daughter's deep sadness. She suddenly realized all her child had lost. This woman said she was unable to forgive her husband and the doctor until she saw that she too had harmed her children. She realized she was giving her children an angry, bitter mother who hated their father. She knew what her daughter needed most was a happy, loving mother who had forgiven her father and the doctor. This woman told me she decided she could no longer force her innocent children to pay the price for the abuse she had suffered. Through the process of personal repentance, she was given the ability to forgive and love those who had abused her. For the rest of her life, her children were blessed with a happy, loving mother who forgave both their father and the doctor who had made a tragic mistake.

It is hard to forgive, but it's so much harder not to forgive. The ability to forgive is one of the gifts of the Atonement. When we don't forgive, we arrest our spiritual development and often remain at the same age emotionally and spiritually as when the abuse occurred. Our body may grow old, but we remain injured children lacking the ability or the necessary tools to deal effectively with life's adult challenges and opportunities. When we refuse to forgive, we limit our ability to develop mature and loving present relationships. As long as we refuse to forgive, we remain victimized children, lacking the ability to experience true empathy. We know the gospel principle of forgiveness in our head but don't experience it in our heart. When we forgive, we open our hearts to more hurt and pain—but we also open our hearts to more peace and joy.

When we forgive, we let go and let God be the judge. Sometimes it appears to us, from our limited perspective, that those who abused us are not suffering for their crimes. We may conclude that God isn't fair or just and that we need to step in and be the person to set things right or cause the offender to suffer. Yet being a true disciple of Jesus Christ requires that we take a different road. If we truly want inner peace, we have to pay the price by living a righteous life. Peace comes when we desire to do God's will more than our own. Being a true Christian means we seek to do good always, even when evil has been done to us. True discipleship invites us to shift our focus from our pain to loving others and understanding their pain. Though it seems contradictory, we heal best when we focus on assisting others. In addition, we heal faster when we primarily concern ourselves with our relationship with God and whether or not we are obedient to commandments and sacred covenants. We will not primarily concern ourselves about what others are saying or doing.

Happiness eludes those who choose not to forgive. "It takes neither strength nor intelligence to brood in anger over wrongs suffered, to go through life with a spirit of vindictiveness, to dissipate one's abilities in planning retribution. There is no peace in the nursing of a grudge. There is no happiness in living for the day when you can 'get even.'"[2]

It is not always possible for us to understand why things turn out the way they do in this life. We may never know until after mortality why we were abused and why many of our righteous desires were not fulfilled. Yet we can be absolutely assured that if we keep the commandments and honor our covenants, everything that happens to us will be consecrated to our ultimate good in the eternities.

BALANCING JUSTICE AND MERCY

As we attempt to forgive, there is a vital need to balance both justice and mercy. In matters of abuse, justice typically comes before mercy, requiring an honest inspection of what has happened. The purpose of examining what has happened is to determine whether the actions, not the people, are good or evil. Justice also asks us to gather evidence about the effects of the abuse. We need to face reality with a balanced perspective that takes into account our own contributions to the problem, along with the contributions of others. However, justice does not require that we assume blame for sins we haven't committed or that we seek control over decisions we have no control over.

Justice requires that we do not deny or exonerate actions when they are dangerous, destructive, cruel, abusive, or painful. To forgive without recognizing the true nature of the offense closes doors to the important realities pain can open. To attempt to be merciful in the absence of justice is to deny the characteristics that make God, God.

I once received a telephone call from an angry woman who was in great pain. Her stepfather had murdered her mother and stepbrother and then had committed suicide. "I will never, never forgive that man," she said. "He has taken my entire family away from me for the rest of my life. I hope he goes to hell. Everybody in the Church tells me I have to forgive him. I refuse. That monster ruined my life."

Sometimes people who are trying to help those who have been wronged tell the person in great pain they must quickly forgive and forget. This overly simplistic solution often leaves the abused person feeling very much alone in his grief. When we want to help others who are grieving, it may be more helpful to acknowledge the depths of their agony and give them time to work through their feelings and the long-lasting consequences of their problem before we offer simple solutions to their deep pain. The person who seeks to heal must first acknowledge the evil, live with all the consequences, choose to come to the Savior, and then—in time and after much more pain—choose to forgive. Forgiveness doesn't require a victim to accept the abuser's actions and doesn't deny the serious consequences of sin.

The principle of mercy follows the principle of justice but cannot rob it. Mercy allows peace to come to the forgiving person as he enlarges his understanding of all contributors to the problem, takes positive actions on his own behalf, and extends to others the mercy he would claim for himself. The person who forgives leaves to God the sorting out of ultimate responsibility, intentions, circumstances, and agency.

THE MIRACLE OF FORGIVENESS

Those who have been abused do not have to wait for the abuser to repent before they can gain access to the miracle of forgiveness. The Savior calls, "Come unto me, all ye that labour and are heavy laden, and I will give you rest. Take my yoke upon you, and learn of me; for I am meek and lowly in heart: and ye shall find rest unto your souls. For my yoke is easy, and my burden is light" (Matthew 11:28–30).

Some victims mistakenly believe forgiving the abuser somehow lets the perpetrator off the hook or condones the sin. Forgiveness takes the victim off the hook. God knows that as long as victims refuse to forgive, they are stuck in their progress toward healing. Some victims also mistakenly believe that forgiveness means they must resume a relationship with the abuser. All healthy relationships must be built on trust. Trust is earned. There will always be cases when it's not safe for the victim to have a relationship with the abuser.

President Gordon B. Hinckley counseled: "If there be any who nurture in their hearts the poisonous brew of enmity toward another, I plead with you to ask the Lord for strength to forgive. This expression of desire will be of the very substance of your repentance. It may not be easy, and it may not come quickly. But if you will seek it with sincerity and cultivate it, it will come."[3] Peace follows forgiveness. The healing that follows forgiveness brings a peace and joy that cannot be found any other way.

FORGIVENESS AFTER THE ABUSER DIES

Many are faced with forgiving an abuser after the abuser dies. One man said it helped him forgive his dead father when he wrote a letter to him detailing the abuse he suffered and the effects it had on his life. Then he took the letter and burned it. As he watched the smoke trail up into the sky, it became his symbol of letting go of his pain. Another man told me he was most helped by transforming the weekly sacrament into a truly worshipful experience where he humbly asked God for help to forgive his mother. As the water touches his lips, he imagines the power of Christ's Atonement like Niagara Falls coming to his aid. As he imagines the Savior's suffering, he knows he is not alone and that someone understands and can comfort him. One woman shared with me that she found it helpful to confront her abusive father, who was represented by a chair. She poured out her soul and expressed every repressed emotion. Then she left the room and left the symbol of her abuser. She closed the door and walked away literally and figuratively. Another woman said she found it helpful to write down her experiences and the effects they had on her life. Then she taped the paper to a helium-filled balloon and let it go. As she watched the balloon rise higher and higher in the sky, she allowed herself to let go of the pain.

None of us has a life without pain or heartache, frustration and loss, yet we can have inner peace. Through the trials of mortality, we learn there is no joy without sorrow, no pleasure without pain, no light without darkness, no sin without forgiveness, no health without sickness, no life without death, and no peace without problems. Peace comes as we move forward, knowing God, like the headlights on our car, will light the way ahead just enough to keep us safe and keep us moving along the road to perfection. Peace comes unexpectedly as a subtle feeling of wellness in spite of the trials of life.

UNDERSTANDING THE ATONEMENT

The Atonement is the greatest opportunity for a meaningful ending to every life story. The Atonement provides the only way to accomplish a permanent change of self. "Jesus had not finished his work when his body was slain. . . . When will he? Not until he has redeemed and saved every son and daughter of our father Adam that have been or ever will be born upon this earth to the end of time, except the sons of perdition. That is his mission."[4] Over and over, Jesus calms our fears. His comforting words are for all: "Fear not, little children, for you are mine, and I have overcome the world, and you are of them that my Father hath given me; and none of them that my Father hath given me shall be lost" (D&C 50:41–42). When our all and the Savior's all come together, we will know Christ because we will be like Him. "That ye may become the sons of God; that when he shall appear we shall be like him, for we shall see him as he is; that we may have this hope; that we may be purified even as he is pure" (Moroni 7:48). The gospel doesn't prevent pain—it heals pain. The Atonement is what makes life worth living.

One man described how God's tender mercies helped him heal from the injuries of an abusive father this way:

> Even though I couldn't have a relationship with my father for most of my life because of his decision to continue abusive behavior, I was able to come to a place of personal peace. I'd come to believe most of his cruel behavior was about what happened to him, not who he was. Sometimes you can't believe just what you see, hear, and experience; you have to believe something deeper. I felt deeply that my father was a son of God. I believe when you push past the boundaries of experience and move into forgiveness, God will reveal to you the beauty of the eternal soul.
>
> I helped dress my father's body before his viewing after he died. That's when I noticed, really for the first time, how small his body actually was. He'd always seemed so large and menacing to me because I'd spent most of my life feeling my pain, not his. As I gently combed his fine, white hair, I thanked him for giving me the chance to be born. I realized his body was just a shell for his soul and that my father's soul was infinite and priceless. As I stood next to my father's casket under the soft lights of the funeral home, it occurred to me he might have found it almost impossible to live to his fullest capacity because of his own difficult childhood. As the son of divorced parents, he also grew up in an abusive home. I wondered who he was before the events in his childhood had scarred him. He seemed like a bird with a broken wing, fallen too soon from the nest. I resolved that day to learn something from my painful past—something that would teach me what it truly means to love and be loved. I longed to bind up the deep wounds of those who went before and those who would follow. Yet I fully understood that healing my family would not be something I could do, but something only God could do.
>
> The last time I saw him alive, it was a day before he died. I heeded an urgent, unexplainable prompting to visit him. When I arrived, he was sitting in a wheelchair eating popcorn and watching television in his bedroom. We talked for a while then suddenly he became agitated and ordered me to leave. I walked from the bedroom into the hallway feeling like I'd just been slugged—again. Then I stopped, took a deep breath, and bowed my head. I realized I was allowing my father's behavior to determine my feelings and actions. I took back my power and prayed.

"Heavenly Father, teach me how to love him."

Then the answer came, "Forgive him. Speak the truth in love." I knew what the truth was for me. The wounded feeling I held deep inside lifted. I opened my eyes, then turned back toward my father's bedroom door. When I arrived at the entrance to his bedroom, I saw my father sitting in his wheelchair rigid and stiff, his eyebrows lowered, with a dark and menacing countenance. I walked back toward him and knelt directly in front of him so we could be on the same level. I waited until he gave me his full attention, looked him in the eye, and then smiled.

"I love you, Dad," I said.

Surprised by my unexpected response, Dad stared at me, confused. His eyes filled with tears. That was our last touch, our last conversation, and the last time I'd see my father alive. His quick passing wasn't expected. Yet, it was the last time. The last moment I had with my father while he was in mortality wasn't the perfect Hollywood farewell scene, but it was enough. No lingering bitterness remained inside me for my father. It didn't matter any more what he had done or said or hadn't done or said. What mattered, what I had any power over, was this: I loved him. All resentment was left behind like old, worn-out clothes that didn't fit me anymore. I understood you can love someone deeply even if they don't have the desire or capacity to love you back. The miracle of the Atonement had gently healed my broken heart, bound my wounds, given me the ability to love and forgive, and graced me with abiding comfort and peace just as Christ had promised. It felt as though a huge burden lifted, and I was free to move forward with my life with renewed enthusiasm and joy.

GOD KNOWS US BY NAME

Just as God called an unschooled, fourteen-year-old boy "Joseph," so are we known by name. God knows our heart. No other relationship in this life even comes close to the Savior's commitment and devotion. God doesn't take away our burdens, but he increases our strength and endurance to bear them. The Atonement strengthens, lifts, comforts, and renews as it also redeems and exalts. "For the mountains shall depart and the hills be removed, but my kindness shall not depart from thee, neither shall the covenant of my peace be removed, saith the Lord that hath mercy on thee" (3 Nephi 22:10). It is our responsibility to draw on the power of the Atonement. We are not alone. "For I will go before your face. I will be on your right hand and on your left, and my Spirit shall be in your hearts, and mine angels round about you, to bear you up" (D&C 84:88). There is no wound that reaches deeper than the healing effects of Christ's love. No matter what we've been told or experienced, love wins in the end. Love always wins.

NOTES

1. David E. Sorensen, "Forgiveness Will Change Bitterness to Love," *Ensign*, May 2003, 12.
2. Gordon B. Hinckley, "Of You It Is Required to Forgive," *Ensign*, June 1991, 2.
3. Ibid., 5.
4. Joseph F. Smith, *Gospel Doctrine* [Salt Lake City: Deseret Book, 1939], 442.

Chapter Fourteen

LEARNING HOW TO LOVE AGAIN

L earning to love is the crowning achievement of life. Yet there are several complexities concerning love that are difficult for abuse survivors. Many who have been harmed by the cruelty of others experience an intense inner struggle concerning love. For example, many people maintain an abusive relationship with someone because they love them and they are a member of their family. If we work through and resolve this struggle, a second remains. Many people are afraid to risk loving someone again after being hurt. Resolving this inner battle eventually gives us the freedom we need to become a genuinely loving person.

Survivors of abuse are often confused about the nature of love. Many abusers claim to love their victims. If victims believe them, their perception of love is a lie. This great lie concerning love also causes many abuse survivors to feel they must tolerate cruel behavior. Family members often put pressure on each other to maintain relationships that are harmful and dangerous. We are all responsible to create a safe and loving home for ourselves and our children. It is entirely possible to love someone even after we have made the necessary decision to no longer have a relationship with them for our own safety and well-being.

One woman told me about her adult, drug-addicted brother who couldn't hold a job because of his violent and explosive anger. Even though this woman was married, with a young family of her own, her mother kept insisting she allow her brother to live with her.

"If you really love your brother, you would not abandon him," her mother said. "He's sick. He needs your help." So this woman allowed her brother to live in her home. She couldn't sleep at night or relax during the day because she knew her brother and his friends were capable of harming her and her young sons. When I suggested that she ask her brother to leave and report his drug-selling activities to police, she asked me, "How can you get your own brother in trouble without feeling guilty?"

I told her that her brother was already in trouble. Holding him accountable for his actions while he still had an opportunity to change and repair some of the damage he'd done was not an act of betrayal—it was an act of love. Most people are confused about how to love an abuser. A victim's genuine feelings of love and fear concerning an abuser are often manipulated, twisted, and distorted by the perpetrator or other family members. It helps to reeducate ourselves on the true definition of love.

One way to define love is the effort we put forth to nurture someone's growth and well-being. Love is a commitment and thoughtful decision to actively assist someone's growth and progress toward God. Love is what we do that promotes spiritual, physical, and emotional development. If we allow someone to abuse us, we are limiting our—and their—personal growth. We are also confused about the true nature of love if we don't encourage an abuser's improvement and accountability. When we don't encourage these things, we are not fully demonstrating love.

When we hold an abuser accountable for his behavior, it is because we love him and trust in the power of the Atonement. When we love an abuser, we believe he is capable of better behavior. We do not underestimate his potential, and we give him opportunities to change and improve. We seek to promote what is beneficial for his development. When we allow an abuser to continue abusing without consequences, he has no reason or motivation to change.

We don't have to harbor hateful feelings in order to hold an abuser accountable. Some have a false notion that in order to be a good person, we need to loyally and silently stand beside our family member in everything—even abusive behavior. Standing beside an abuser makes us a collaborator or enabler. Careful consideration must be given to the harm that is happening to children if we don't deal with abusive relationships while impressionable young people are in our home. Many children have as hard a time forgiving the parent who did nothing as forgiving the one who perpetrated the abuse.

Abusers lie when they tell their victims that if they truly love them, they will not abandon them. The loss of a relationship is a natural consequence of abusive behavior. Abusers often lecture victims on their desperate need for unconditional love and threaten horrible consequences if the victim leaves. Some abusers apologize profusely and promise the abuse will stop. Abusers can be very convincing. Most see the victim as the cause of their behavior instead of looking inward. All survivors of abuse need to know this: when we love an abuser, we allow them to experience the full consequences of their behavior every time.

PROTECTIVE ARMOR

Most adult survivors of childhood abuse spend a lifetime looking for ways to feel worthy, accepted, and loved. To soothe our repressed pain, we develop one or more kinds of protection to shield ourselves from further injury. The behavior that served us in childhood later becomes our prison walls as adults. If we used defenses such as illness, compulsive thinking, anger, violence, self-hatred, or withholding affection to protect ourselves from further assault when we were children, we may unconsciously repeat those same destructive thinking patterns or behaviors as adults. Even when we're free from abuse, we often continue living our lives as if we still need to protect ourselves. As a result, we often end up recreating the kind of life we experienced as a child and hoped to escape. We remain controlled by past, unresolved family issues.

If we were abused as children, we learned that if we love someone, we'll be hurt or betrayed. So we develop habits of withholding our affection from those around us, afraid to have our hearts broken again. If we do this, we eventually become the unloving spouse or parent we experienced as a child. When we withhold our love, it seriously damages everyone. While it may give us the illusion we are protecting ourselves from further rejection and pain, we are in fact creating new rejection and pain for those who come after us. Someone has to feel the pain of not having their love reciprocated, move on to healthy relationships, and then decide to love again. We can't let the pain and disappointment over others' inability to love us rob us of the joy and satisfaction that we can have from loving our spouse and children today.

Love needs to be demonstrated. We can feel love for our children, spouse, and associates, but until we express it in tangible ways, they will never know it or feel it. When we withhold our love we remain cut off from ourselves and from God. Everyone needs nurturing, encouragement, and physical affection nearly as much as they need food. If we don't know how to love, we need to become students of the Master.

WHAT LOVE IS

Love is an act of courage, especially for victims who have loved once and been burned. Because survivors of abuse have been betrayed, abused, or abandoned, they've learned that loving someone causes pain. It takes childlike trust in God for abuse survivors to risk loving someone again. Offering our love is a gamble, yet it is a risk most of us are willing to take because we've loved before and everything turned out all right. Loving someone can be terrifying for an abuse survivor. They have loved before and everything did not turn out all right.

Truly loving someone changes us at our very core and allows us to feel true joy. After healing, abuse survivors realize the test of our love is not the response we received, but the quality of love we offered. Even though we have been rejected, betrayed, left, hurt, or disappointed, after healing, we come to understand that true love never fails us as long as we choose to give it. Even when our love is not reciprocated, it flows back to us and fills our heart with peace. All the love we've ever felt is alive and well in our hearts, whether or not it was ever returned.

Love is life and light. Love literally casts out darkness and fear. "I am come that they might have life, and that they might have it more abundantly" (John 10:10). Abuse survivors have had past experiences that bind fear, pain, and darkness to their previous efforts to love. After making the choice to maintain only healthy, loving relationships, abuse survivors can experience an abundant life full of light, joy, and peace. When we free ourselves from destructive relationships, we also free ourselves to love again. We develop courage after experiencing overwhelming fear and inner light and peace after enduring profound darkness and evil. An abundant life is a personal choice to experience a genuinely loving relationship with God. As we experience real love from a divine source, we are less likely to be deceived by imposters. All of us can learn to love and be loved. We are all worthy of love.

Love is appreciating someone's value. We truly love someone when we see their eternal worth in the eyes of God. Many abuse survivors have never felt valuable. Only God can endow us with an indestructible sense of our divine worth. When children grow up knowing they are loved and valued, they enter adulthood with a security no one and nothing can take away from them. When children grow up not being loved and valued, it is much more difficult to acquire deep-seated feelings of being lovable or valued later in life. The natural man cannot give himself this inner sense of priceless value alone. We need our Creator to open our eyes to the infinite worth of every human soul, beginning with our own.

LEARNING AND PRACTICING LOVE CODES

Abuse survivors often don't know what normal, healthy, loving behavior is because they've never experienced it. It helps to think of the expression of love as a kind of secret code between two people. Everyone has specific ways that help them feel loved. Some people like to be told "I love you" vocally. Some people appreciate gifts. Others enjoy quality time alone with heartfelt conversations or love letters. Some people feel loved when family members perform acts of service and prove to be trustworthy. Others feel loved most when they are physically hugged, kissed, and caressed. When we become students of love, we search for ways to offer our love in the secret code each individual understands and appreciates most. When we

149

are a student of love, the way someone loves us becomes less important than the quality of love we offer.

Sometimes it helps to better understand love by learning what love is not. Love is not demanding, self-absorbed, dramatic, selfish, jealous, or needy. Love is not manipulative or controlling. Love is not forced, fake, or focused on making a good impression. Love is not fearful, unsatisfied, critical, intolerant, negative, judgmental, proud, devious, pious, or greedy. There is a difference between mature love and an unhealthy emotional attachment. Desperately needing someone to be with us so we don't have to be alone is not love. Longing for someone to fill our unmet needs is not love.

Many abusive families function under this unspoken rule: "I'll reject you before you reject me." Each family relationship is constantly scrutinized and manipulated to suit the purposes of self-absorption, selfish motives, and self-pity. Unhealthy family members hold back affection, backbite, talk negatively about each other, manipulate, choose favorites, and give to get. Unhealthy families actively seek to undermine or diminish each other. Can abusive families change? Yes. All positive and enduring change in a family begins one person at a time.

GROWING IN LOVE

We are each given a legacy by our parents—their love for each other and us or the heavy burden of their lack of love for each other and us. Yet we always choose what we will do with what we are offered. Like a pebble thrown in the ocean of time, our choice to love or not to love our spouse and children will change our life, change their lives, and change the world. When we approach the end of our lives, will we regret long years wasted on marital complaints and family feuds? Will we realize we missed opportunities to develop our own ability to love because we wanted to be right or punish someone? Will we regret not fully experiencing all the joys as well as the sorrows in our family relationships? Will we have done the work to really love someone?

We can't afford to waste a lifetime waiting for someone to finally love us after we've been abused. Somebody has to love first, and because we have no precious life to waste, that somebody has to be us. If we have trouble demonstrating our love because of our past, we can learn and we can change. First we resolve to involve ourselves only in healthy relationships. Then we proceed to practice. Love can be expressed physically, emotionally, spiritually, and vocally. We develop healthy relationships by concerning ourselves more with the quality of love we offer than the kind of love that comes back to us. Selfless love will flow outward to our children and our grandchildren, blessing the lives of our posterity forever.

Nothing that can happen to us will destroy us if Christ is alive in us. "It is upon the rock of our Redeemer, who is Christ, the Son of God, that ye must build your foundation; that when the devil shall send forth his mighty winds, yea, his shafts in the whirlwind, yea, when all his hail and his mighty storm shall beat upon you, it shall have no power over you . . . because of the rock upon which ye are built, which is a sure foundation, a foundation whereon if men build they cannot fall" (Helaman 5:12).

EXPERIENCING GOD'S LOVE

Our ability to love is a gift from God. We can love because we've been loved. "Herein is love, not that we loved God, but that he loved us" (1 John 4:10). To experience God's love, we must first become acquainted; a price must be paid. We all have the capacity to learn how to love because God and Jesus Christ first loved us. Divine love is the only love that never falls short of expectations. It is through their infinite love that we are given the capacity to love. We pay the price to experience God's love through obedience to the commandments and through living in companionship with His Spirit.

If we depend on other mortals to feel loved, we will always be disappointed and disillusioned. When we focus on receiving God's love for us, and then share that love with others, love will never fail us. Will the love we offer always be returned? No. Abuse survivors know full well that would happen only in a perfect world, and this is not a perfect world. Yet love is never lost, for even when it is not reciprocated, it pours back into the heart of the person who loves, and it softens and purifies the soul. A pure heart is one that has been broken and then healed through the Atonement.

Because of the love of God, we can transcend a loveless childhood or marriage. "Eye hath not seen, nor ear heard, neither have entered into the heart of man, the things which God hath prepared for them that love him" (1 Corinthians 2:9). Filled with God's love, we become more compassionate through pain, courageous by facing our fears, strong as we repent of our weaknesses, forgiving as we forgive, and generous as we bless others' lives. God's love for us is personal and real. When we feel God's love, we have the opportunity to share what we've experienced with others. Whether or not those we love choose to love us in return is up to them.

LETTING GO AND LETTING LOVE

I remember falling through the metal poles on a piece of playground equipment when I was young. I reached out and grabbed hold of a bar so I wouldn't fall all the way to the ground and get hurt. I dangled there for a long time while several of my classmates tried to convince me to let go. They told me I wasn't that far from the ground, but I didn't believe them. I dangled there until my trembling arms finally gave out. Then I fell—roughly two inches—to the ground. I felt foolish for being terrified when I was perfectly safe. Similarly, when we have been hurt, we long to love and be loved, but we're afraid to be vulnerable because we don't want to be hurt again. If all we've known is pain from relationships in the past, being close to someone else can be frightening. So we hold fast to a secure railing, ever ready for a reason to turn back, protect ourselves, change our minds, or take back our love. Because we've learned that love hurts, we are suspicious and unsure of others' motives. If we want to experience true joy, we need to let go and receive the love of God.

Whether or not even one other human being ever loves us has nothing to do with our eternal worth. Our worth is separate from the love that's offered by other mortals. The love others offer to us is contingent on their agency. The love we give is contingent on our agency. The love of God surpasses everything others have to offer. No matter what we think of our selves or others, God always thinks better. God knows everything about everyone, and He loves all of us anyway. We are all worth infinitely more than we can possibly comprehend; we are literal children of God. In partnership with our Creator, there is no end to what we can become.

One woman described how she felt when she knew her marriage was over but her love didn't have to end. She said she had been married for twenty-five years when her husband told her he had been unfaithful. The news was a crushing blow. She wanted to go into counseling and do everything in her power to preserve the marriage. Her husband wanted to stay married while maintaining his relationship with the other woman. She described her feelings this way:

> I didn't divorce my husband because I hated him; I divorced my husband because I loved him. I could not live the immoral lifestyle he wanted me to live without breaking my covenants with God, who I also love. I could not live that way and still love me. So I had to let him go. I didn't have to let go of my love for him.

WHERE TO FIND GOD'S LOVE

Feeling God's love for us, feeling love for ourselves, and feeling love for others is an interwoven circle. Those who have been abused often fear that loving again will bring only pain. Like a child who has had his hand burned on the stove, we learn to stay away from stoves. We hold back love and we measure and allot our outgoing love to meet the incoming—always keeping score, suspicious, careful, watchful, and ready to be hurt again. Life gets colder and colder when we love like that. Our reticence and aloofness soon become loneliness as we push others away.

Loving someone takes the courage and faith of a child, literally leaping into the unknown and trusting that God will catch us. The greatest fear in love is that it won't be returned. It is possible to love others deeply even when they don't love us back. God's love will compensate for all we lack. We have a choice to make. We can remain safely holding onto the railing, holding our love tightly to ourselves, or we can decide to let go. Is it worth the risk to love someone if that love was once betrayed or never returned? Do we step into vulnerability without anything to hold on to? Do we open our hearts to the chance of more pain? Do we take the leap of faith to love someone when there are no guarantees? Yes! "There is no fear in love; but perfect love casteth out fear" (1 John 4:18).

Interestingly, God doesn't just love us first but also commands us to love Him back. "Thou shalt love the Lord thy God with all thy heart, and with all thy soul, and with all thy mind" (Matthew 22:37). God also commands us to love ourselves and each other. "Thou shalt love thy neighbor as thyself" (Leviticus 19:18). Jesus also tells us to love those who do not love us: "Love your enemies, bless them that curse you, do good to them that hate you, and pray for them which despitefully use you, and persecute you" (Matthew 5:44). Why are we commanded to love our enemies? God wants to bless us with peace. We can't have peace when we hate someone.

TRUSTING GOD

Sometimes those who have experienced abuse act like my young children when I'm attempting to teach them to float in the water for the first time. I stand in the swimming pool holding them up and tell them to relax. "I'm right here next to you," I say. "Now put your ears back into the water and stretch out. There now, relax and trust the water to hold you up. You'll be okay. I'm right here." Often my children don't trust me; they thrash about, causing themselves to sink. If they relax and listen, they quickly learn how to float. "Relax and breathe," I say, positioning my hands beneath my child so there is no chance he can sink. "I'm here. Now wave your arms gently back and forth. Now kick your feet."

The children who listen to my voice and trust me float easily and move through the water with gentle ease. Those who are too afraid sink like a rock and require many, many more lessons. We're all like that. God is standing right next to us. Quietly he whispers, "I'm here, right next to you. Relax, breathe, and trust me. Now repent. Now forgive. Now love." If we listen and trust, we can relax knowing God is ever present and will not let go or let us down. Sometimes when times get hard, I picture myself with the Savior's loving hands beneath me, ready to catch me when my strength gives out. God is ever ready to offer each of us one more lesson. Even when I thrash about, make mistakes, and lose faith, I know those arms are still gently cradled just beneath me. God's love is always there; we need only to receive the Atonement to feel it. So we have a choice to make. We can retain our false sense of emotional safety by hoarding our love, or we can focus on the quality of love we have to offer. The only safety in love is feeling God's love for us and offering it to others.

BREAKING DOWN CHILDHOOD
DEFENSES AND DISTORTION

Childhood victims of abuse develop defense systems for protection from anxiety and pain and often use this same defense system in adulthood. One childhood defense is blaming the victim. For example, if you witnessed your mother abusing your sister when you were a child, you may have demonized your sister and idealized your mother—or in other words, you told yourself your sister deserved your mother's abuse. That perception helped you cope as a child. Perhaps you were secretly relieved that your sister was the one who was being hurt instead of you. You never allowed yourself to feel your sister's pain or your guilt for not comforting her. You may have let yourself believe that you deserved the superior treatment you received from your mother. For those reasons, you grew up with a distorted reality of your sister, always taking your mother's side, judging your sibling as unworthy of anything good. You find yourself wondering why your relationship with your sister is strained. If you go back to your childhood experience and realize your sister was innocent and abused and you did nothing to help her, you will realize your sister did not deserve the treatment she received. You will also realize that it has been your superior attitude toward her that has made it hard for you to love her.

For another example, if one parent was unfaithful or abandoned us physically or emotionally as a child, we may grow into adulthood subconsciously afraid our spouse will be unfaithful or abandon us. We become manipulative, controlling, and jealous for reasons that have nothing to do with our current spouse and everything to do with our childhood. We may play a major role in re-creating the family pain we hoped to avoid. In short, when we are aware of what we did to protect ourselves from the pain of being unloved as children, we can begin to live life as mature human beings and stop blaming other people.

HEALTHY WAYS TO DEVELOP SELF-LOVE

An empty vessel has no water to share. With all the demands of living, we need to allow ourselves regular time for healthy self-love. Here are a few suggestions:

Put first things first. Our first priority should be to love God and personally feel God's love for us every day. Then we can receive the gifts of the Atonement.

See ourselves through God's eyes. When we see this way, we shine like children do.

Come unto Christ. When we repent and forgive, Christ is alive in us.

Find our personal mission. God needs us to bring love to his sons and daughters. How we do that is an essential part of our personal mission.

Recognize our self-worth. Our value as a son or daughter of God cannot be diminished by anything others do or say.

Don't confuse worth with worthiness. Our divine worth is something that can never be diminished or destroyed. Worthiness can be worked on.

Forgive. Forgiveness frees us to live in the present.

Develop loving friendships. True friendship provides a way to give and receive love.

Value our time. Time is the one great equalizer. We all have twenty-four hours a day. We need to choose wisely and do less with more love.

Learn to simplify. Cutting back on demands and responsibilities isn't easy, but it's vital.

Remember healing is a journey, not a destination. We must detach ourselves from negative thoughts and emotions and allow God to guide us home.

Respect the physical body. It is important to eat nutritious food, get adequate rest and exercise, and learn to relax and meditate.

Take time to develop talents. Everyone needs a way to express themselves. Talents are gifts we receive from God to bless others.

Teach. God wants us to share what we've learned.

DEVELOPING THE CAPACITY TO LOVE

The good news is that we can all learn how to love by practicing. We can turn from God, but God never turns from us. We are never alone. The power of the Atonement is always available to us. In partnership with Deity, all individuals can heal. "I can do all things through Christ which strengtheneth me," Paul wrote (Philippians 4:13). The law of the harvest is eternal. The light of Christ, along with the tears of mortality, will provide the sunshine and rain for the tender seeds of love to grow. If we plant seeds of love, then charity will be our harvest.

The gospel of Jesus Christ is hope. That includes the hope that we can learn to love and be loved. Then this hope grows to faith and faith to charity. If we have charity, it will be well with us. "Now abideth faith, hope, charity, these three; but the greatest of these is charity" (1 Corinthians 13:13). One of the greatest possible missions in life is to completely devote ourselves to another human being in love. There are many roads to travel if we want to create something that will last beyond our short lifetime on earth. But perhaps children who have known what it feels like to be loved by us will be our most lasting legacy.

Chapter Fifteen

HEALING THROUGH
THE ATONEMENT

We support people who have suffered a death in their family. We allow them to be depressed, sad, and angry as they work through the grieving process. Those who have experienced destructive relationships have also suffered a tragedy—a loss of innocence, trust, love, and self-confidence. Yet when someone is abused, often no one around them wants to face the issue, hold the abuser accountable, or help the victim grieve and work through the healing process. Most people avoid abuse issues or pretend they don't exist. Those who have been abused are often encouraged to suppress their pain and told to quickly forget and forgive. These cultural traditions keep abuse survivors in pain and far from healing.

In our culture, we tend to hide scars, especially the wounds caused from abuse. I find it comforting that the Savior's first physical act in the Book of Mormon was to stretch forth his hands and show the people his scars—the symbols of his sacrifice for us. He was not embarrassed or ashamed that he was wounded by those who might have loved him. Jesus asked each person there to come forward one by one and thrust their hands into his side and feel the prints of nails in his hands and feet. At first the people didn't know who He was. When they understood, they fell down and worshipped him. (3 Nephi 11:17).

Healing is not a quick and painless procedure with an exact recipe for everyone to follow. Healing comes as we continue on an individual journey to come to Christ.

One woman described an unexpected moment of divine healing this way:

> Several years before my mother's death, my father took an early retirement, and my parents moved to a house near my home. Dad often needed help with yard work and mother's physical care during the final years before her death. During the last two years of her decline, Mom gradually lost control of her mental capacities, muscles, and bowels. My husband was a bishop and seldom home. I was the mother of many very active, busy teens; it was a challenging period of life for me.
>
> Dad sometimes asked me to watch Mom while he ran errands. The last time I watched Mom at my house, she had an embarrassing accident and called me into the bathroom to help her. It took over an hour to clean her up and wash and dry her clothes. I still remember the look in her eyes and the childlike way she reached for my help with the most intimate matters. She was horribly self-conscious; I did my best to put her at ease. Though Mom was mortified, I found the tender experience gently healing.
>
> "It's all right, Mom," I said, placing my palm against her soft cheek to reassure her.
>
> My mother broke down and wept, huge tears dripping down her cheeks and pooling onto her blouse. The whole experience felt unexpectedly sacred to me. The simple voluntary physical act of cleaning up the mess she'd made helped to heal a deep wound in my soul from the abuse I'd suffered at her hand. I still remember the clear water from the sink washing the stains away and the shaft of light from the window reflecting off the tears in my mother's eyes. As I knelt in front of her helping her redress, I kissed my mother's toes and washed her feet with my tears. Though I never would have guessed, loving and serving my mother in the last, most dependent years of her life was a healing balm for my soul and perhaps even for hers. I was able to see her as a vulnerable child of God and care for her in intimate ways that sanctified any residual pain left from my past dark memories.

Most of us know who Jesus Christ is and perhaps even love Him. Yet many of us haven't experienced how He saves and redeems us personally. We will not come to know Jesus as our Savior until we have felt our own personal need to be saved. President Boyd K. Packer said, "The Atonement of Jesus Christ is the very root of Christian doctrine. You may know much about the gospel as it branches out from there, but if you only know the branches and those branches do not touch the root, if they have been cut free from the truth, there will be no life or substance nor redemption in them."[1] It is the great Jehovah who is the wounded Jesus, the Savior of mankind. Jesus wears the scars, wounds, and evidence of His love. Each week as we take the sacrament, we are given the symbolic physical emblems of His suffering. These symbols of the blood and body of Christ should shock and humble us.

CLEANSING THE WOUND

When one of my children falls down and skins her knee, I know from past experience what has to happen next if the injury is going to heal properly and completely. If I allow my child's screams not to touch the injured knee to keep me from scrubbing and disinfecting the damaged site, healing will be delayed and my child will be in for a lot more pain in the future. My injured child will grab my hands and do her best to keep me from touching the wound as I turn on the water. If I go easy and try not to touch the injured site, the dirt or gravel will remain in the wound and later develop into an infection that prevents healing. If I'm insistent and carefully scrub the scraped knee, the injury will heal much more quickly and completely. Even after the necessary cleansing process, my children scream again when I try to apply the antibiotic ointment before I bandage the wound.

Though I'm being helpful and loving, it doesn't appear so to my children because what I'm doing hurts. Though I make calm and soothing comments like, "Let me help you. Let me wash away the dirt so your sore can get better. Let me apply this ointment to keep the germs away," my children are seldom soothed in the moment of crisis. I am not appreciated. In fact, my children yell some pretty negative comments directed at me. I wouldn't put myself or my little ones through the whole ordeal if I didn't know for certain what I was doing for my child was ultimately loving and compassionate. We're all similar to my screaming children after being hurt, wanting God to give us relief from pain but not willing to go through a thorough cleansing or renewing process because we already hurt and we don't want to hurt anymore. So we foolishly delay our submission to a higher and loving power who is trying to help us. We effectively fight off the application of a soothing ointment and clean dressing. Sometimes we complain to God in bitterness for letting the bad thing happen in the first place, while we willfully hold back the very hands trying to help us clean the wound and apply the healing ointment. God is not the cause of the awful things people do to each other. The gospel of Jesus Christ does not prevent pain—it heals pain.

We can't move forward in healing from emotional, physical, and spiritual wounds if we blame God and resist the very person who is trying to help us. When we refuse God's help because of our limited perspective, we choose to remain in a state of pain, hurt, loneliness, anger, and bitterness. That state of being is a self-imposed hell. Our part in personally partaking of the Atonement of Jesus Christ is in trusting that we will be healed by our loving Creator and given the desire and power to love after we repent or forgive.

Healing comes like Christ's blessing of the little children in the Book of Mormon—one by one. We can find peace in this life knowing that God, who loves us best, knows precisely what we need. Sometimes healing may mean that the burden or pain is actually removed, but more often healing comes as increased strength, courage, patience, assurance, guidance, support, or understanding to bear the challenges and burdens we are given. Trusting in God's will, timing, and manner of healing allows our loving Creator to cleanse us from all deep wounds. When we submit our will to His, we are given the desire and ability to repent and forgive, which in turn endows us with the capacity to love. With the capacity to love we become new, reborn to the light of God's love and Christ's healing Atonement. After doing all we can do, it is God's love and the Savior's Atonement that saves, heals, and exalts us.

We all face heartbreaking circumstances that give us deep pain. Each difficult experience invites us to heal so we can deal with our pain in a way that will not permanently harm us or those who come after us. If we do not do the difficult work of healing in this life, we will pass down to successive generations the pain that was handed to us. Healing is a lifelong journey, so we need to be patient with ourselves as we move forward. We can know that we're never spiritually alone. "I will never leave thee, nor forsake thee" (Hebrews 13:5).

THE HEALER

If we think we are suddenly going to have a loving relationship with someone who abuses us, we are in denial. It is easier to live in denial than face the truth and feel pain. Facing reality and feeling pain is the only way to heal. I hate to go to a doctor's office, but there is one thing that can get me through those doors—pain. Most of us, when we are in enough pain, will do almost anything to stop our suffering. The greatest physician, the ultimate healer, is Jesus Christ. "He hath sent me to bind up the brokenhearted, to proclaim liberty to the captives, and the opening of the prison to them that are bound" (Isaiah 61:1). Jesus Christ will heal our wounds, wipe away our tears, and love us completely. We will remain in spiritual, physical, and emotional pain until we access God's love through the Atonement. There is nothing, absolutely nothing, we've experienced that our Savior does not understand. "He descended below all things, in that he comprehended all things, that he might be in all and through all things" (D&C 88:6). Jesus did not experience just the sinner's pain—he experienced the victim's pain as well, as He confronted and experienced every human trial. He bore the burdens, grief, heartaches, physical pains, and depression of the entire human family. "And he cometh into the world that he may save all men if they will hearken unto his voice; for behold, he suffereth the pains of all men, yea, the pains of every living creature, both men, women, and children" (2 Nephi 9:21).

Most of us believe in Jesus, but we haven't personally experienced how He saves and redeems us. When my young son faced his second surgery in a year, what frightened him most was being told he had to fast before the operation. So my husband offered to fast with him. Because of my husband's offer, my young son was better able to face what was most difficult for him because he knew he didn't have to face it alone. Though we feel separated from God in mortality, we are never truly alone. Because of the Savior's Atonement and mortal experience, He knows how to succor us. Because God loves us, we're allowed the necessary life experiences to help us develop our character. We can call on God whenever we desire so that we can do this together.

STAGES OF HEALING

Healing from abuse and betrayal, like grieving after a death, often comes in stages as we work through the process of coming fully to Christ. These stages do not generally happen in a neat step-by-step progression, and they generally cover long periods of time as we experience denial and shock, anger and blame, guilt and bargaining, depression and loneliness, and finally acceptance and hope in Christ.

The following list might prove helpful as we work our way through the stages of healing.

1. The first stage is *acknowledging abuse has occurred*. We have to know we've been abused before we can gain insight into the impact abuse has had on our life. At this stage, we have to remember and think about deeply troubling and painful emotions and memories. At this stage, it's important to understand all our reactions are normal.

2. The second stage is *stopping any ongoing abuse and making a decision to heal*. At this stage, we make a commitment to change our behavior concerning the abuse. This may require that we set new boundaries or remove ourselves from an abusive relationship. We may need to place other commitments aside for a while as we fully experience painful emotions, face difficult issues, change our life circumstances, and get loving support from people we can trust.

3. The third stage of healing is *talking*. We need to allow ourselves to talk about the abuse. At this stage, we acknowledge out loud that we were abused and that it was not our fault. It's important to choose a knowledgeable and compassionate person to talk to.

4. The fourth stage of healing is *placing responsibility for the abuse with the abuser*. There are surely reasons people become abusers, but there are no excuses. We can forgive, but we must

not excuse. Excusing is dangerous. We need to understand we are not to blame even if we went along with the abuse.

5. The fifth stage of healing is *feeling all our emotions, including anger.* We are often taught that anger is a bad emotion and should be repressed, but it is part of the healing process if it moves us into positive action instead of retaliation. Anger is a powerful positive emotion if it gives us the necessary energy to finally do something about our oppressive relationship If we direct our anger at the horrible multi-generational consequences of abuse, this emotion can help us learn to be assertive, clear-headed, and strong as we end all our cruel relationships. It takes great courage and strength to work through extremely difficult issues and get rid of all negative or distorted beliefs about self and others. We can't do this without full access to all our emotions.

6. The sixth stage of healing is *dealing with loss and sadness.* We can't heal from something we can't feel. At this stage, there will be many, many tears. Whether it was the loss of childhood innocence, trust, or the loving family we always wanted, healing takes raw courage. We may be afraid that if we start crying, we'll never be able to stop. We will learn that the intensity of painful emotions does pass.

7. The last step to healing is *living fully in the present and working to secure a future without abuse.* At this stage, we are able to accept that abuse is part of our past. We can now acknowledge what we gained from the healing process. It may be self-acceptance, wisdom, respect, inner strength, discernment, confidence, or courage. We've now learned how to protect and nurture ourselvles. We're free to set goals and more forward.

The process of healing feels like a long, dark tunnel with no end in sight. There is a light, and that light is Christ. When we take our broken heart to the Savior, He will comfort us and actually walk beside us in our pain. He has the power to turn darkness into light, anger into forgiveness, bitter into sweet, blame into understanding, fear into faith, and sorrow into salvation. Our Savior understands every feeling of pain and hurt we have experienced or ever will experience, because He has felt it. When we suffer and then choose to come to Him, we have the opportunity to become like Him. We more fully prize what He has done for us. If we come to Christ, we can experience the abiding joy that comes only after experiencing heartrending pain. If we truly desire healing with all our hearts, we can be taught such wonderful things about ourselves, others, and the meaning of life. The Savior truly will be our finest counselor and truest friend as He walks beside us, heals our deepest wounds, and holds us safely in the arms of His love. Jesus said, "Therefore, let your hearts be comforted . . . ; for all flesh is in mine hands; be still and know that I am God" (D&C 101:16).

Nothing a mortal can do to us will have the power to halt our eternal progression. When we access healing through the power of the Atonement, life's difficult experiences sanctify instead of destroy. The painful reality we've been given will not be removed, but we will be healed from the negative personal effects of those agonizing realities. Christ does not only want to heal us—He wants to exalt us too.

LEAVING THE PAST TO GOD

Those who have lived without love know profoundly how important it is for every soul to feel loved. If we come to Christ with our longing for love, He will provide for us all that we lack. Christ's well of understanding has no end to its depth. His ability to comfort has no bounds. His love can heal every private heartache we've known. Though He understands perfectly the eventual positive outcome of all tragedy, still Christ weeps with us. Our Savior has all the time we need to comfort us and provide infinite solace to our souls.

We can't change the past. Even God can't change what happened in the past. When we give up the longing that the past could be different, we open our hearts to the hope that the future can be better. After we've grieved our loveless past, Christ will help us heal so we can provide the love to others that we were denied.

The American Red Cross trains their volunteers to help those involved in trauma focus on how they survived instead of repeatedly going over the ordeal. One important survival skill for abuse victims is flatly refusing to give up hope. We can make a life-long goal to overcome the effects of abuse, even if our present efforts don't seem to be showing any fruits. The desires of our hearts are known to God and are sacred. There is dignity in the struggles of life if we face them with faith and optimism. With the help of God, we can each acquire the audacity to move forward with hope no matter what has happened in our past.

AVENUES TO CONTINUE IN THE HEALING PROCESS

Healing can be thought of as a life-long process instead of a destination. If we want to stay in the process, the following ideas may be helpful:

Taking physical action. We live in a physical world and need to take physical action before we can have a change of heart. When we give to others what we were denied, we allow the flow of God's love to enter our souls. We won't heal if we sit around dwelling on past trauma; we need positive experiences in the present. When we have a new positive physical experience, we can expect that in a few days we will have a new thought or feeling.

Trying something new. Healing and growth are available if we keep learning new things. It's healthy for us to be a perpetual student; it keeps us humble, eager, and in the learning mode. When we try something new, it helps keep us in touch with how it feels during the change process. When we were children, we were constantly learning new things. Adults fall into comfortable routines. We need to keep learning if we want to heal and grow.

Journaling. Writing helps us figure out the complexities of our lives. Writing helps pull us from the jumble of our anxieties and fears and then gives us a broader perspective and clearer view of future possibilities. Writing is therapeutic and can give us a sense of closure. Keeping a journal requires that we think and ponder. Everyone should leave an honest written record of his or her life. Journaling sends a message to those who come after us that we care about them and want to assist them on their mortal journey.

Internalizing positive sayings or quotes. Words are powerful. Those who have been abused should keep positive words or phrases running through their minds all the time. These words serve to bring the mind into the present moment and focus forward in positive ways. Post powerful quotes in strategic places in your house so you see them daily.

Reading. The scriptures will always be a great resource for healing. Abuse victims can find role models in the scriptures. Many characters in the scriptures had to deal with people who abused them. It also helps to think of the scriptures as love letters from God. One useful way to use the scriptures as an aid to healing is to take a question to God and then look for answers in the standard works by checking the topical guide for verses that may provide ideas. Then we can read that verse and others, eventually choosing one to meditate on that day. There are many other good books that offer insight for those seeking to heal. Because each person's experience is unique, it's most helpful to read a variety of self-help books and fiction. The greatest masterpieces of literature were often inspired from the trials of the author. Reading good fiction gives us insight as we experience life vicariously.

Enjoying nature. Being alone in nature can do wonders for soul healing. Looking up at the stars at night, noticing a beautiful sunset, smelling the air after a rainstorm, taking a walk on the beach or in the mountains, growing flowers in our yard—all these connections to nature will help us feel closer to God.

Self-expression. We feel alive when we pursue a personal form of self-expression. Whether we garden, cook, decorate, sew, paint, write, perform music, dance, landscape, sing, or create email family newsletters, there is a divine need to express ourselves.

Children. Children live in the present and are excellent teachers in how to enjoy life. Spending time with children gives abuse survivors an opportunity to relearn liveliness, spontaneity, and playfulness. Children freely offer pure love and acceptance.

Music. Music seems the most pure form of language to our souls. Music gives expression to our deepest feelings and even has the power to lift and help heal the wounds of abuse. Listening to and performing music can alter how our brain and body function. Uplifting or soothing music can aid in healing. Music can comfort, inspire, uplift, and bring peace. Good music can help us heal the deepest parts of ourselves. It is in the spaces between the notes, or the pauses, when we can be taught about our divine nature by a loving and watchful Heavenly Father.

Humor. Sometimes the best therapy is a good laugh. Abuse victims are often ultra-serious and need the reprieve humor can offer. We can collect a library of books or other media that help us look at life lightly. Scientists have discovered that laughter can lower blood pressure, increase muscle flexion, and even trigger a flood of endorphins. Endorphins are brain chemicals that can bring on a feeling of well-being and even euphoria. Laughter also affects our immune system. Gamma-interferon, a disease-fighting protein, rises with laughter. So do B-cells, which produce disease-destroying antibodies, and T-cells, which orchestrate our body's immune response. Laugher can also shut off the flow of stress hormones, the fight-or-flight compounds that come into play when we feel hostility, rage, and stress. Stress hormones suppress the immune system, raise blood pressure, and increase the number of platelets in blood, which can cause fatal artery blockage. Keeping a sense of humor really is serious business.

Healthy habits. Mortality is the time to learn how to make our spirits the master of our bodies. We learn self-mastery as we take good care of our physical bodies with exercise, nutritious food, and adequate rest.

Serving. There is no surer way to heal than by trying to help others. The world is full of precious souls who need our love and understanding. Centering our thoughts on the needs of others puts our pain in better perspective.

Meaningful work. Work keeps us moving ahead in life. Working for others is healing. If we look for ways "to clothe the naked, and to feed the hungry" (Jacob 2:19), we will never lack for meaningful work. When we see the divine in each other and in ourselves and then work to lift and bless each other, we do God's work.

Waiting on the Lord. Healing requires humble patience and the willingness to wait on God's timing. Waiting and enduring well means we move forward with our life in positive ways before we have all the answers to life's tough questions.

Eternal perspectives. Mortal life is but a tiny drop in the endless oceans of our eternal existence. If we accept God's great plan of happiness and trust in the Savior, then adversity can actually be used as a catalyst for personal growth. We won't be overcome by unbearable problems, because we trust that God will make all things right in the eternities. We effectively reframe our perspective when we prayerfully search for opportunities to be taught through the Spirit. The Spirit gives us enlightenment that helps us face the future with abiding faith and courage.

Consequences of moral agency. We all agreed to come into an unjust world. We fought the War in Heaven for the privilege of receiving a body and the chance to choose between good and evil in mortality. This agency would be for our good—if we keep our covenants. When we don't keep our covenants, we have no promise and suffer the natural consequences of our choices. Inpremortal life, we understood the risks and still shouted for joy. We knew we would not be safe from betrayal, violence, abuse, sorrow, death, sickness, or heartache. Yet we understood we would be safe in God's love.

A broken heart and a contrite spirit. Everything we have is a gift from God. The only thing we have to place on the altar is a broken heart and a contrite spirit. God never asks us to do anything that won't bless us. In fact, the whole course of our salvation and our family's salvation depends on our change of heart. One of the best ways to know if we are true disciples of Christ is by the way we treat people, including ourselves. No one can truly love another person without ongoing personal refinement. This purification follows submission to God's will and partaking of the Atonement of Jesus Christ through sincere personal repentance and forgiveness.

Reclaiming baptismal covenants through the sacrament. We have the opportunity to be forgiven or healed every week by partaking of the sacrament. We can experience the fruits of repentance and forgiveness by worthily partaking of the bread and water with a spirit of humility and a new determination to be more Christlike. When we feel the water touch our lips, we allow the "living water" to fill our hearts and give us peace. "Every one that thirsteth, come ye to the waters" (2 Nephi 9:50) and "with joy shall ye draw water out of the wells of salvation" (Isaiah 12:3). When we renew our baptismal covenants every week, we can be made clean from the sins we committed and be healed from those committed against us. Receiving the Atonement changes our conduct. We turn our lives over to God. To know God is to do His will; to know Jesus is to follow Him.

Receiving the Atonement. Because of Jesus Christ, both justice and mercy are fulfilled. No repentant sinner or innocent sufferer will be alone in his suffering. When we understand the Atonement, we will have a spiritual awakening. Every ordinance and principle of the gospel is given to us from God to lead us to the Atonement. When we are yoked with Christ, God accepts our combined efforts.

The difference between trust and love. There is a common confusion about the relationship between trust and love. You can love someone and not trust them. Abusers cannot be trusted.

Positive affirmations, meditation, and self-guided imagery. Deep breathing, progressive muscle relaxation, hypnosis, self-guided imagery, and meditation have been useful for some abuse survivors, as have imagination, affirmations, and redirecting negative thoughts.

Understanding no experience is wasted. Nothing we go through needs to be wasted experience. Every challenge we go through can develop qualities of patience, humility, determination, compassion, and love—if we endure well, with full trust in God. Everything we experience has the capacity to build our character, purify our heart, and make us more charitable. Every hardship refines our spirits.

Avoiding the quicksand of self-pity. Unforgiving people are loveless people; loveless people are self-imprisoned. Self-imprisoned people are not happy and suck every relationship dry. We don't have to be held hostage by those who do not love.

Asking the right questions. Bad things happen to everyone. If we ask, "Why did this happen to me?" we're asking the wrong question. A better question is, "Now that this has happened, what can I learn?" There can be meaning and responsibility in all suffering. An essential part of the meaning of life lies in what we learn from abuse and betrayals. If we suffer and find no meaning, we suffer in vain. We have the power to choose how we respond to any situation.

Utilizing fasting, prayer, and priesthood blessings. Most of the scars of abuse are so deep they require the power of prayer, fasting, and priesthood blessings. "This kind can come forth by nothing, but by prayer and fasting" (Mark 9:29). Priesthood blessings are often overlooked as a path to healing. Blessings can heal our hearts as well as our bodies.

Attending the temple. Regular temple attendance, when possible, will help us receive personal revelation and peace from the cares of the world and give us a connection to God. When we receive our endowment, we have power to overcome the snares of the world.

FEELING GOD'S LOVE

We can't offer love to others if we don't know what it feels like. Filled with God's love, we find ways to bring light, warmth, and joy into all our human relationships. If you've ever been burdened down with the sins of others, you know how heavy life can be waiting for people or circumstances to change. Waiting on the Lord, on the other hand, is not just hanging out in the waiting room in pain, waiting for a chance to see a doctor who's always running late; it is choosing to move forward with the childlike faith that everything will turn out all right in the end. "But they that wait upon the Lord shall renew their strength; they shall mount up with wings as eagles; they shall run, and not be weary; and they shall walk, and not faint" (Isaiah 40:31).

No matter what our circumstances are, life goes on and life gets better, deeper, and richer for those who love God, themselves, others, and the holy gift of life. The way we live our lives will affect many, perhaps millions, in the future. We must never underestimate the power of our influence for good or ill. Our smallest acts of kindness, forgiveness, and charity will ripple out into the universe, touching the lives of those we have never met. Developing a Christlike character and learning to love, in spite of our past experiences, is the most important things we can do with our life.

The good news of the gospel is that we don't have to repeat the negative or unloving pattern of family relationships we have experienced. We are not to blame for the abuse we have experienced, but we are responsible to make sure the negative relationship patterns stop with us. We can't change the past, but we can change the future. We can heal and share with the world the new person we have become and the love we have to give. We've been promised great gifts and empowering aids as baptized members of The Church of Jesus Christ of Latter-day Saints, one of which is the gift of the Holy Ghost, who grants us essential guidance and sustaining love from the other side of the veil. Jeffrey R. Holland said, "You have help from both sides of the veil and you must never forget that. When disappointment and discouragement strike—and they will—you remember and never forget that if our eyes could be opened we would see horses and chariots of fire as far as the eye can see riding at reckless speed to come to our protection. They will always be there, these armies of heaven, in defense of Abraham's seed."[2] We can ask for divine help any time of the day or night; we are not alone. We will receive the strength necessary for the battles we fight or the load we carry.

COMING TO CHRIST

All of us have hurts, disappointments, fears, and scars from a variety of injuries. Though largely unknown to others, our pain is known by One who will always encircle us in the arms of His love. "Behold, I am Jesus Christ, the Son of God. . . . I am the light which shineth in darkness. . . and I will encircle thee in the arms of my love" (D&C 6:21, 20). Healing through the Atonement gives us a crystal-clear view of reality that comes when we are willing to look at ourselves and others through God's eyes. That means we are endowed with charity, which enlightens our awareness, understanding, compassion, and respect. God can open the windows of heaven to our household and teach us how to love each other. Families don't heal until individuals heal. Gospel principles and ordinances aid in personal healing when one soul decides everyone deserves to be treated with respect and love.

NOTES

1. Boyd K. Packer, "The Mediator," *Ensign*, May 1977, 56.
2. Jeffrey R. Holland, "For Times of Trouble," *New Era*, Oct. 1980, 15.

Chapter Sixteen

FINDING MEANING IN PAIN

Why do we have to experience pain? Because God gave man agency. Death, sin, heartache, disease, accidents, betrayal, disaster, suffering, abuse, and a hundred other causes of pain are all part of mortality. Bad things happen to all of us, even when we're trying to do what's right. Still, we have been promised that everything we experience in this life will be consecrated to our gain if we keep our covenants with God. No matter what happens, we are given this promise: "Search diligently, pray always, and be believing, and all things shall work together for your good, if ye walk uprightly and remember the covenant wherewith ye have covenanted" (D&C 90:24). In essence, life is hard—and then, if we endure in righteousness and receive the blessings of the Atonement, we are exalted.

Perhaps one reason we suffer more than we "need" to is that we have a preconceived idea about how our life should play out, and then we are disappointed when events don't turn out as planned. We can rest assured that everything that happens can be a catalyst to personal enlightenment and growth if we choose to submit to God's will and receive the gifts of the Atonement. Accepting all life experiences with gratitude and humility requires that we think about our trials in a different way, that we step outside our pain and see our experiences from an eternal perspective. When we attach our will to God, we eliminate much of our suffering because we trust the Creator's wisdom more than our own. Though our trials may seem unbearable, we can know we will be ennobled by those circumstances if we accept all things with childlike trust in God's ultimate plan for us. When we fully receive the gifts of the Atonement, we stop looking around the corner for some perfect life that is always outside our reach. Once we truly experience the love of God, no one is our enemy and there is nothing more we need.

One woman told me she was angry at God for years. All she had ever desired was an eternal family, but her husband had abused her and their children and then left her for another woman. She said one day it dawned on her that God had not abandoned her; she had abandoned God. She was going it alone even though her Heavenly Father was always there, waiting and willing to help. She had not yet felt her own personal need to be saved from the effects of sin, because she felt the sins she was suffering from were not her own. This realization came to her one night when she looked up at the stars in quiet desperation.

"Where are you, God?" she asked defiantly. "I've done everything you've told me to do. Where are the blessings you've promised?"

Her answer came suddenly and powerfully as she gazed into the night sky. She realized the stars in the heavens were always there, even during the day, but their light and beauty were revealed only in darkness. In a similar way, she understood God's love was always there. His promises for her joy and happiness had not changed. If she let go of the past, God's most brilliant love would shine forth in her darkest hour. At this moment of enlightenment she fully understood her personal need for Jesus Christ to be her Savior.

"My circumstances didn't change," she said, "but I changed the way I thought about my life. I realized I needed to be saved from the effects of sin just as desperately as my ex-husband. I fell to my knees and pleaded with Jesus to help me. I became a true Christian that night."

Another reason we suffer is that we're prisoners of the way we think. Instead of seeing things the way they really are, we see things the way we really are. We create our own private heaven or hell with our thoughts. Whether we feel joy or pain sometimes has less to do with our circumstances than with how we perceive them. Choosing to receive the gift of the Atonement liberates us from misery to happiness, from bondage to freedom, from retribution to repentance, from fear to forgiveness, and from cruelty to compassion. How we respond to life's heartaches determines our destiny. Everything can be taken away from us except the freedom to choose our attitude. All personal suffering diminishes when we form a clear picture of the meaning we derive from our pain.

WHY IS PAIN PART OF GOD'S PLAN?

Pain, if we choose healing through the Atonement, can prepare our hearts to receive all the blessings God has in store for us. Before we came to this earth, we agreed to our present mortal conditions. We knew life here would be unfair. We understood innocent people would suffer. Now that we're here in mortality, why do we doubt God's wisdom in our behalf? We've been promised our experiences will redeem and sanctify us—if we come to Christ through repentance and forgiveness. Nothing that happens to us by the choices of others prohibits us from any blessing promised by God—if we remain obedient and faithful.

Pain, if we choose healing, produces qualities of patience, faith, humility, and courage. Experiencing pain invites us to purify our hearts and expand our ability to love and be loved. Pain gives us the opportunity to become more compassionate and tender. Adam eloquently sums up the point of mortality when he says, "They taste the bitter, that they may know to prize the good" (Moses 6:55). Deep understanding and compensating peace come only after the trial. When we experience evil at the hand of others, it can become our personal refiner's fire—where our impurities are burned away as dross. Nowhere is it written that life is supposed to be a smooth celestial highway with no accidents or road blocks. Mortality is designed for us to experience the tension between good and evil, light and darkness, sickness and health, life and death. Pain is our greatest teacher if we want to learn. The Atonement will not fail us. Christ is the perfect solace for our souls.

NEW LIFE

Childbirth can be described as an ocean of pain that ebbs and flows like waves. At the crest of each wave, the labor pain is at the peak—then it gradually subsides. There is a small break between waves, where the laboring mother is allowed to regroup and then brace herself for the next pain. The closer she gets to actually giving birth, the closer the waves of pain come together. When the mother is actually delivering a new child, the pains don't have any break between them. That's when the mother wonders if she can hold on any longer. But she does—and because she does, new life is born. God knows we all need to be reborn, given new life through pain, whether emotional or physical or both. When we really become new, when we develop a new heart and a rebirth of purpose, it always follows the most difficult times—the peak of pain when there is no letup, when we think we can't go on. But we do go on. So we are reborn many times in life, reborn to joy—all following great pain.

We all have certain expectations from life. What matters more than what we expect from life is this: What does God expect of us? If we will ask for, listen to, and then act on our impressions from God, our lives will have meaning and purpose under any circumstances. God invites us to choose betterment over bitterness, growth over self-pity, and inner peace and joy over jaded attitudes. Hell is self-absorption. Heaven is other-absorption. So we choose. What kind of a life do we want here in mortality and in the eternities?

THE PROMISE OF PAIN

We experience pain because there is no other way to develop wisdom, humility, charity, and endurance. Without pain, we would never be compelled to ponder the vital questions of life. When God presented the plan of salvation, we shouted for joy because we wanted this mortal experience; and it wasn't because we were naïve. We understood that mortality, even with all the problems, would provide us with experiences that would help us acquire knowledge and wisdom. Experiencing mortality was the only way for us to continue our eternal progression and become like our Heavenly Parents. Each experience, if we choose to receive the gifts of the Atonement, teaches us to more completely trust the love of God.

Pain often provides the vital key that unlocks our understanding. The realization of impending death gives us necessary incentive to take loving and responsible action now. Knowing that this life will end is what makes being alive today so sweet. Pain, then, is a disguised gateway to joy. Happiness is always waiting on the other side of tragedy. Only through painful experiences can our hearts break and then be put back together by a loving God; only through pain can our blind eyes be healed to sight again, our confused thinking given new understanding, and our waning strength be replenished with oceans of new power. When we are in the midst of new sorrow, it does not seem that joy will ever come again. But it does. If we turn to God, the sun always rises, spring follows winter, and new life and joy always follow pain—always.

When we understand the magnitude of the Savior's sacrifice for us, we realize nothing has more significance or worth. If we're obedient, we can return to our Heavenly Father changed, improved, ennobled, and sanctified because of our experiences in mortality. We are promised that we will never be given a challenge in this life that is beyond our capacity to bear with God's help. One of the greatest secrets about pain is that having gone through the refiner's fire, there is nothing left to fear. Though it appears a paradox, without suffering and death there is no joy and life. The abiding peace that follows our deepest pain is one of the tender mercies God made available to all who love Him.

Because of pain, we can all more fully appreciate what Christ endured in Gethsemane. The Savior understands and can comfort us because he has felt it. Christ knows all anguish, depression, betrayal, and loneliness. Christ knows intimately the private anguish of every abused son or daughter of God, for He has experienced every heartache, physical pain, burden, and fear of the entire human family. "Surely he hath borne our griefs, and carried our sorrows" (Isaiah 53:4). We are never alone.

FINDING MEANING IN PAIN

One way to find meaning in pain is to learn something from our difficult experiences that we can use to bless someone else. When we reach outside the narrow confines of our own pain by serving others, we are better able to put our challenges into perspective. We are not the only ones in need of love. When we serve without expectation of reward, we open our hearts to the compensating blessings promised to all who love and serve God.

Another way to give meaning to our pain is to allow difficult experiences to wake us from the slumber of complacency and ingratitude. Every morning when we wake from the seeming death of sleep, every sunrise after a long dark night, every spring after the coldest winter can help us see the promise of the Atonement in everything. When the Master's gift has touched our lives, we no longer walk sightless in a world of miracles. We can then choose to humbly accept our winters of pain as well as our springs of joy. Everything we go through will guide us into a better future if we choose love over hate. No power on earth can take away God's love.

Another way to find meaning in pain is by applying the healing balm of gratitude. Focusing on blessings invites the Spirit. This life is only a small drop in eternity, and God has promised us that everything will be equitable in God's time and way. No one can do anything to us that will last for eternity. We are the only one who can affect our eternal progression permanently. So we have a choice—we can be bitter, or we can call on our God to strengthen and heal us. The choice is ours.

Still another way to find meaning in pain is by allowing our heartache to increase our appreciation for the Savior and what He experienced. Much of the blood Christ spilt in Gethsemane was from the pain of the innocent. "And he shall go forth, suffering pains and afflictions and temptations of every kind; and this that the word might be fulfilled which saith he will take upon him the pains and the sicknesses of his people" (Alma 7:11).

Sometimes in the midst of great personal anguish we are moved to ask, "Is there no other way?" The answer is that there is no other way—if we want to learn the difference between good and evil, have seed and the joy of our redemption, and receive the eternal life that God gives all who are obedient (Moses 5:11). The state of Adam and Eve was described as

> having no joy, for they knew no misery; doing no good, for they knew no sin. But behold, all things have been done in the wisdom of him who knoweth all things. Adam fell that men might be; and men are, that they might have joy. And the Messiah cometh . . . that he

may redeem the children of men from the fall. And because that they are redeemed . . . they have become free forever, knowing good from evil; to act for themselves and not to be acted upon. And they are free to choose liberty and eternal life, through the great mediator of all men or to choose captivity and death. (2 Nephi 2:23–27)

What was true of Adam and Eve is true of us. If we hope to have joy, we must also know misery. If we hope to do good, we must also have the potential of doing evil.

HIDDEN TREASURES

There are great hidden treasures of wisdom to uncover from all the pain we experience. One treasure is that as our hearts heal, they fill with great stores of love. With that love, each of us has beauty to create, responsibilities to perform, and people to cherish. We need access to our courage and peace of mind to fulfill our mission in this life. All suffering we experience prepares us to open our hearts to God and to each other. How can we mourn with others if we've never mourned ourselves? How can we lift another unless we've needed lifting and understand what they need? Out of the fiery furnaces of our life we can choose to come forth, polished with light.

It has been said that pain is inevitable, but suffering is optional. Likewise, pain is inevitable, but becoming Christlike through suffering is optional. No experience we have needs to be wasted; everything we experience has the potential to teach and refine us. We can be made holy by our trials. There is a rich pattern and deeply meaningful purpose to each individual's life. Instead of focusing on all we've lost through trials, we can choose to celebrate all we've gained.

Meekness allows us to trust that there is a purpose and sacred meaning to all life's experience. Elder Neal A. Maxwell said:

> Human suffering does not automatically produce sweetness and character unless meekness is present. Meekness is the mulch that must go in the soil of adversity in order for empathy to grow and in order for character to grow. Jesus could not have become the most empathetic person had he not been the most meek person. . . .
>
> The thermostat on the furnace of affliction will not have been set too high for us—though clearly we may think so at the time. Our God is a refining God who has been tempering soul steel for

a very long time. He knows when the right edge has been put upon our excellence but also when there is more in us than we have yet given. . . . Righteous sorrow and suffering carve cavities in the soul that will become later reservoirs of joy.[1]

The gospel of Jesus Christ is not insurance against pain but rather an infinite resource to help us deal with pain. God can and will make all things work together for our salvation if we are obedient and faithful to our covenants. We are free to choose—not what happens to us, but how we will respond. Instead of asking, "Why me?" when we experience trials, sorrow, loss, and abuse, it may be more helpful to ask questions such as these: "After all I've lost—what remains?" "Now that I have been harmed, how do I heal?" "Because of this experience, what does God require of me now?" "What can I learn so I can bless the lives of others?"

LEARNING TO TRUST GOD

Though we become adults in mortality, we are still children in the eyes of God. Our divine Creator has infinite patience for us as we learn and grow. It's like we're in this great big "Sunbeam class" for godhood, struggling with even the most basic principles. Don't hit each other. Don't steal each other's things. Don't be jealous of each other. Be kind. Wait your turn. The Master lovingly pleads, "Behold, ye are little children and ye cannot bear all things now; ye must grow in grace and in the knowledge of the truth. Fear not, little children, for you are mine, and I have overcome the world, and you are of them that my Father hath given me; and none of them that my Father hath given me shall be lost" (D&C 50:40–42).

The scriptures reassure us that, in time, everything will work toward our good. Individuals who have endured abuse or any other great tragedy have the same potential to reach exaltation as those who have not. Individuals and families will become stronger or weaker after experiencing abuse, but they will never be the same. Individuals who willingly and consistently use gospel principles as a part of their recovery and healing process will receive this glorious promise: "But they that wait upon the Lord shall renew their strength; they shall mount up with wings as eagles; they shall run, and not be weary; and they shall walk, and not faint" (Isaiah 40:31). Perhaps the sweetest, most comforting words in the scriptures for those who have experienced abuse are these: "To appoint unto them that mourn in Zion, to give unto them beauty for ashes, the oil of joy for mourning, the garment of praise for the spirit of heaviness. . . . The Lord . . . hath sent me to bind up the brokenhearted, to proclaim liberty to the captives, and the opening of the prison to them that are bound; . . . to comfort all that mourn." (Isaiah 61:3, 1–2). Broken hearts, captive spirits, and those that mourn—all these are the consequences of abuse. The Atonement will not eliminate pain, yet Christ provides a watchful companionship and applies the balm of Gilead to every broken heart.

Healing from abuse can prepare our hearts to serve others. Every morsel of love and service we send out into the world will be returned to us a hundredfold. Pain invites us to come to Christ so that we can regain the personal power and peace of mind that evil robbed from us. Because of the Atonement, we can experience the "peace of God, which passeth all understanding" (Philippians 4:7). That is God's promise. God never breaks His promises.

Everyone has a mission to fulfill in this life. After we heal from abuse, we can champion a cause greater than our personal pain. The more we give ourselves to a great cause or a person, the more Christlike we become. The courage to face our painful circumstances and rise above them gives us the opportunity to become the sons and daughters of God we were meant to be. Our Savior does not want only to redeem us but also to exalt us. The moment when we feel most alone may be when God is most with us. Remember Joseph Smith at Liberty Jail when he pled, "O God, where art thou?" (D&C 121:1).

The inspiring revelations the Prophet received after that desperate plea were preceded by great heartache and abuse. Even Christ cried out to God in agony on the cross just before His grand mission was fulfilled, "My God, my God, why hast thou forsaken me?" (Mark 15:34). We too can rest assured that at the very moment when we are unable to bear anymore, God is there. "For a small moment have I forsaken thee; but with great mercies will I gather thee. . . . I hid my face from thee for a moment; but with everlasting kindness will I have mercy on thee, saith the Lord thy Redeemer" (Isaiah

54:7–8). To all our pleas for deliverance from our pain, God answers, "My son [or daughter], peace be unto they soul; thine adversity and thine afflictions shall be but a small moment; and then, if thou endure it well, God shall exalt thee on high" (D&C 121:7–8). "The Son of Man hath descended below them all. Art thou greater than he?. . . Therefore, fear not what man can do, for God shall be with you forever and ever" (D&C 122:8–9).

MEANINGFUL SURVIVAL

We are survivors of abuse if we are alive. Meaningful survival, however, is something more. Meaningful survival means we not only triumph over suffering, but we also take our knowledge and experience and put our new understanding into action to help someone else. Meaningful survival is not just getting on with our life, but forever leaving the victim role and choosing a different road. Meaningful survival means we take responsibility for our present and future life by resolving any resulting damage to us psychologically, physically, emotionally, or spiritually that is still harming our potential and growth or our ability to love. Meaningful survival means taking back our power and moving boldly into the future without fear. Meaningful survival is developing the ability to use our gifts to empower and educate others. Meaningful survival means we understand God loves abusers and victims equally. Meaningful survival allows us to leave judgment to God and gives us the assurance that our Heavenly Father will also be merciful to us all.

Meaningful survival means we don't need to punish or hurt ourselves or the abuser outside the demands of justice. Meaningful survival means we look for the pain—not the power—in the abuser, see their pitiful condition, and feel compassion for their consequences.

THE GOOD NEWS

God's prescription for healing is individualized for each of us. The gospel of Jesus Christ does not spare us from abuse, but it gives us a way to overcome the negative effects of abuse. Through the Atonement, we are given a way to heal from something that could destroy us. Because of difficult experiences, we come to understand that life has deep and sacred meaning and responsibility under any circumstance. God can turn any pain, suffering, or sickness into joy. "They that sow in tears shall reap in joy" (Psalm 126:5). A loving God knows we learn from pain. "And ye shall be sorrowful, but your sorrow shall be turned into joy. . . . And your heart shall rejoice, and your joy no man taketh from you" (John 16:20, 22).

The Atonement can quite literally mend broken hearts and homes. President Boyd K. Packer testifies, "Restoring what you cannot restore, healing the wound you cannot heal, fixing that which you broke and you cannot fix is the very purpose of the atonement of Christ."[2] The actions of others can never destroy us; we only destroy ourselves by our response. "Acts may cause pain, anguish, even physical harm, but they cannot destroy your eternal possibilities in this brief but crucial life on earth. . . . Your attitude can control the change for good in your life. It allows you to have the help the Lord intends you to receive. No one can take away your ultimate opportunities when you understand and live eternal law."[3] Hope is our anchor. "Even when the winds of adversity blow, our Father keeps us anchored to our hope. . . . He will 'consecrate [our] afflictions for [our] gain.' Even when our trials seem overwhelming, we can draw strength and hope from the sure promise of the Lord: 'Be not afraid nor dismayed . . . for the battle [is] not yours, but God's'"[4]

Bread Maker Parable

One day, I walked into the kitchen and found my two-year-old in the biggest toddler mess of the century. He'd dragged out all my huge, ten-gallon buckets of sugar, rice, flour, and macaroni and was diligently scooping the sugar into the rice and the rice into the flour. Before I could open my mouth and ask what in the world he was doing, he glanced up at me. He was standing in a billowing cloud of white, covered from head to toe with a fine layer of flour dust—except for his two brilliant blue eyes staring up at me.

"Look, Mom," he said proudly, "I'm the bread maker!"

That's when it dawned on me what my son was doing. He was trying to be like me. Whenever I made bread, I got out all those big white buckets and started scooping. As I looked at my son basking in his natural disaster, my heart melted like butter in the sun. How quickly my misunderstanding of his motives changed to a deep and tender appreciation of his desires. How much I loved him for trying. It didn't matter to me that he didn't know what he was doing, that he'd been unsuccessful, or even that he'd made a horrible mess of things. His childlike effort was enough.

I know God sees us with infinite compassion, even when we're unsuccessful or make a mess of our lives. I know Jesus is there to help us clean up and loves us for trying. I know Christ will make up the difference between where we are today to where we need to be to return to the presence of God. From the deep stirrings of love I feel for my children, I have a small glimpse of what God feels for me and for every one of us. Each soul is priceless. God understands and appreciates our small efforts. Though often unknown to others, all our heart's desires are known to God.

No form of abuse can prevent us from receiving even one single blessing God desires to give us. God's divine design for each of our lives will be fulfilled in God's time and way. What we choose to do with pain will determine the quality of our lives. Joseph Smith said, "I never could have felt as I now do, if I had not suffered the wrongs that I have suffered. All things shall work together for good to them that love God."[5]

We are never alone. We have been promised, "I will go before your face. I will be on your right hand and on your left, and my Spirit shall be in your hearts, and mine angels round about you, to bear you up" (D&C 84:88). We are not asked to grit our teeth and bear it. We are asked to trust God and be joyful. "In the world ye shall have tribulation: but be of good cheer; I have overcome the world" (John 16:33). Our willingness to wait with patience and hope for answers to life's most difficult questions is the evidence of our deepest faith and trust in God. We are required to offer our discipleship, obedience, will, and covenants kept. The rest is in God's hands.

Often I've stepped outside into a gray, rainy day and looked up at the heavens when there is no light and everything seems dreary and bleak. Yet I know the sun is behind the clouds and when the storm passes, the brilliant rays will bathe the world in light. "The cloud of darkness shall be removed from overshadowing you" (Helaman 5:41). The Savior of the world is behind the dark days of our lives. Through the Atonement, he will bathe our souls with light and love, even in the midst of all the raging storms of life. When we become true disciples of Jesus Christ, we receive God's love. This love can come directly from Him or through other mortals who serve Him.

There is absolutely nothing more important to us than the Atonement of Jesus Christ. Nothing. Our Lord and Savior did for us what we cannot do for ourselves. The infinite Atonement is a miracle, cause for rejoicing, and reason for deep personal gratitude and reverence. No matter what we've done or what others have done to us, we can experience the joy Alma speaks of: "Oh, what joy, and what marvelous light I did behold; yea, my soul was filled with joy as exceeding as was my pain!" (Alma 36:20). We have so much to hope for. There is always hope where there is love. Together with our Lord and Savior, we can overcome all challenges and heartaches in this life.

"Each of us will have our own Fridays—those days when the universe itself seems shattered and the shards of our world lie littered about us in pieces. We will all experience those broken times when it seems we can never be put back together again. We will all have our Fridays. But I testify to you in the name of the One who conquered death—Sunday will come. In the darkness of our sorrow, Sunday will come. No matter our desperation, no matter our grief, Sunday will come. In this life or the next, Sunday will come."[6] As we hold our heads up, open our arms, and walk boldly into the light of God's love, we will be healed. May we offer each other our most tender reassurance and assistance on our mortal journey. May we find deep, abiding peace in knowing God's love is always there. As a loving parent comforts a weeping child, God whispers to all of us, "Be still, and know that I am God." (Psalm 46:10).

NOTES

1. *The Neal A. Maxwell Quote Book*, edited by Cory H. Maxwell (Salt Lake City: Bookcraft, 1997), 208, 7, 335.
2. Boyd K. Packer, "The Brilliant Morning of Forgiveness," *Ensign*, Nov. 1995, 19–20.
3. Richard G. Scott, "Healing the Tragic Scars of Abuse," *Ensign*, May 1992, 31–32.

4. Joseph B. Wirthlin, "Cultivating Divine Attributes," *Ensign*, Nov. 1998, 27.

5. *History of The Church of Jesus Christ of Latterday Saints*, 7 vols., edited by B. H. Roberts, 2d ed. rev. (Salt Lake City: The Church of Jesus Christ of Latterday Saints, 1932–51), 3:286.

6. Joseph B. Wirthlin, "Sunday Will Come," *Enisign*, Nov. 2006, 30.

Appendix

ABUSE DEFINITIONS

Appendix

ABUSE DEFINITIONS

A buse victims often have a difficult time setting boundaries for acceptable behavior in their relationships with others. Setting boundaries is the way we become a friend to our self. Boundaries define limits. We all need to be able to tell others when they are acting in ways that are not acceptable to us. We have both the right and the responsibility to protect ourselves from abuse. The following definitions and descriptions may be helpful to those who are learning to set healthy boundaries to keep themselves and others safe.

VERBAL ABUSE

Verbal abuse is any language used to manipulate, control, ridicule, put down, insult, label, humiliate, belittle, vilify, or show disrespect or disdain for another. Verbal abuse also includes making threats, name-calling, constant criticism, yelling, sarcasm, condescending remarks, and telling jokes that embarrass or demean. Verbal abuse includes cursing, accusing, blaming, exaggerating, and fabricating, along with finding humor at the expense of another. We can destroy the spirit of a child or an adult by the words we speak without ever laying a hand on him. Words can build or destroy, uplift or humiliate.

MENTAL AND EMOTIONAL ABUSE

Mental and emotional abuse includes any attitude or behavior that interferes with another person's healthy development. Mental and emotional abuse is any behavior that injures, harms, or unnec-essarily controls another. Blatant disregard of another's opinions, abilities, or skills, or consistently and consciously withholding approval, praise, love, or acceptance are also forms of emotional and mental abuse. Threats or blackmail (to harm self or victim), exposing someone to unnecessary risks, abandoning someone in a dangerous place, refusing to help when someone is sick or injured, or preventing someone from seeking medical care because it might be used as evidence against the abuser are also forms of mental and emotional abuse. Attempts to control every aspect of another's life, including but not limited to finances, food, social contacts, and transportation are also mental and emotional abuse. Harassment, lies, false accusations, and contradictions used to keep the victim off-balance and confused are also mental and emotional abuse. Making threats or actions that destroy property or belongings, harming or killing pets, and throwing objects are all forms of mental and emotional abuse. Using children as weapons of war against a spouse and letting children into private marital arguments are forms of mental and emotional abuse. Withholding communication, shelter, food, or affection as a form of control, punishment, or manipulation; acting in a dictatorial way; and humiliating family members or associates is also emotional abuse. Refusing to express loving feelings and ignoring or minimizing another's feelings is emotional neglect.

Adults who do not live in the same home can still emotionally and mentally abuse other adults, including family members. Harassment or stalking is defined as any course of conduct that conveys physical, verbal, or written threats (direct or implied) to individuals that cause the victim to fear bodily injury or experience emotional distress to themselves or members of their family. Stalking includes repeated pursuit or surveillance, uninvited entry into a home, destruction of personal property, and using harassing phone calls, letters, or emails. Harassment also includes attempts to publicly defame the victim by spreading lies to the victim's friends, employers, Church leaders, and neighbors. Harassment or stalking can also be a form of abuse perpetrated by past dating or marriage partners.

Rejection and abandonment constitute the ultimate form of mental and emotional abuse. Failure to step in and protect a child when a parent or sibling is doing or saying abusive things is collaborative emotional and mental abuse. Refusal to provide adequate praise, encouragement, interest, or time can be a form of emotional and mental neglect that is often underestimated for the damage it causes. Failure to protect a child when a spouse or another child is doing or saying abusive things also is emotional and mental neglect.

PHYSICAL ABUSE

Any intentional assault to our body is abuse and causes physical, emotional, and spiritual pain. Physical abuse is inflicting nonaccidental bodily injury on another person and includes, but is not limited to, locking in closets, binding, shaking, hitting, biting, burning, slapping, scratching, squeezing, beating, throwing, shoving, choking, kicking, punching, and acting in any other way to cause harm. Physical abuse may come in a single episode or repeated episodes. An intentional injury that requires medical treatment is severe physical abuse. Creating a climate of fear and withholding resources necessary for a healthy life are also forms of physical abuse, as is allowing a child to witness a parent physically abusing another sibling or spouse. Severe spanking by using belts, switches, or any other weapon of torture is also physical abuse. Even though this kind of abuse may be accepted in some cultures in the past or present, it is not an acceptable form of discipline for disciples of Jesus Christ. Physical neglect includes withholding affection and failure to provide adequate medical care, basic education, nutrition, or protection from the elements. Insufficient supervision or guidance is also a form of physical abuse, as is abandonment.

SEXUAL ABUSE

Human intimacy should be used within the bounds of the law of chastity, which restricts sexual relations to husbands and wives who are legally and lawfully married. Sexual abuse occurs when someone sexually exploits another person in order to satisfy his or her own needs. Sexual abuse is any form of sexual activity with a child by an adult; it is also any form of sexual activity with a child by an adolescent. Seeming consent is not an issue: by moral and civil law, children are not able to consent. Sexual abuse includes the use of persuasion, enticement, or coercion to engage a child in any sexual conduct. Sexual abusers often use a position of trust or the victim's vulnerability to induce a child to participate in sexual activity.

Sexual abusers can be boys and girls or men and women of all ages. Sexual abuse interferes with the normal and appropriate development of sexuality and can be a one-time event or a series of progressive involvements. Sexual abuse in any form is a direct violation of the laws of God and the laws of our society.

In most areas, incest is defined as sexual abuse of a child by a family member, including a birth, adoptive, step, or foster parent, grandparent, brother, sister, aunt, uncle, or first or second cousin. Incest is probably the deepest family wound. Incest is any sexual activity between a child and another family member, whether or not the child is aware of what is happening. Incest often involves threats to the victim.

When incest occurs, there is a powerful temptation to find a quick cure, but this short-circuits the healing process. Every family member is seriously harmed when incest occurs and needs help even if they are not the one who was sexually violated. Incest perpetrated by an adult almost always requires excommunication and legal consequences. Incest causes additional problems because the sexual abuser lives in the home, so the victim often has no support and may be blamed for the breakup of the family when the perpetrator is asked to leave.

Sexual abuse also includes any sexual experience within the marriage covenant that is demeaning, forced, or unacceptable to either partner. Sexual abuse between husbands and wives includes inflicting pain, using force or intimidation, and persisting in doing things during times of sexual intimacy that a partner clearly communicates is painful or offensive. Spousal sexual abuse also includes withholding sexual intimacy as a form of punishment or as a means of control or manipulation.

Persons who view or become addicted to pornography are going outside the marriage covenant to satisfy their sexual needs. Many pornography addicts feel compelled to act out what they have seen. Intimate sexual conversations or behavior with persons outside the marriage in online chat rooms, on the telephone, or in person are also a form of sexual abuse.

Parents, older siblings, or spouses can emotionally sexually abuse family members when they make derogatory sexual remarks about their own or their child's or spouse's body. Emotional sexual abuse also involves inappropriate bonding, such as making the child the parent's confidant about intimate matters in the marriage. When a parent is closer to a child than the parent is to his or her spouse, the child is being forced to meet the parent's intimacy needs, which often constitutes emotional sexual abuse. Emotional sexual abuse also takes place when a parent or another adult teaches a child that his or her body and sexuality are dirty or shameful. Emotional sexual abuse takes place when a mother or father fears or hates the opposite sex and contaminates the child's feelings about men or women. Emotional sexual abuse includes teaching boys about nocturnal emissions and girls about menstruation in a way that makes the child feel scared or shameful. Children should be taught that the human body is beautiful and that the changes that occur during puberty are natural and desirable. Every child should be taught to love and respect his or her physical body.

Sexual abuse also involves exploitation of a child or spouse by taking pornographic pictures, using family members for prostitution, or exposing spouse or children to patently inappropriate movies, jokes, language, magazines, or Internet material. Children may also be exploited with gifts, special favors, or the promise of a special position in the family in return for sexual favors. Abusers use these techniques to hook the child into taking responsibility for his or her involvement with the abuser and produce unearned guilt in the victim. Any unwanted inspection of private body parts or intrusion (excluding for normal medical and hygiene care) is also sexual abuse.

Sexual neglect also includes boundary violations. Parents should lock their bedroom door to prevent their children witnessing the parents' involvement in intimate activities. Parents should also respect their children's privacy boundaries in an age-appropriate way when parents or children are bathing, dressing, undressing, or using the bathroom. Sexual neglect can include not teaching children in a healthy and age-appropriate way the proper names for private body parts, the purpose and beauty of intimate relations between husband

and wife, and what changes to expect with approaching puberty, menstruation, and nocturnal emissions.

A child or adolescent who sexually abuses others should be investigated as a possible sexual-abuse victim who is acting out what he or she has experienced. Some teenage abusers have had previous involvement with illicit media or pornography. An increasing number of perpetrators today began as pornography addicts who later acted out what they saw with siblings, cousins, or neighbor children.

Sexual abuse is never the victim's fault, and victims should never be told they caused or encouraged the abuse. No one should minimize the seriousness of sexual abuse. Those who have been sexually abused often need professional help. Incest attacks the foundation of identity. Victims have learned not to trust other people—not even themselves.

DATING PARTNER ABUSE

Adolescents and adults need education about abuse in dating relationships. We need to teach both males and females to guard their chastity and not be manipulated or touched in any way that does not show respect. We need to teach our children they don't owe their dating partner anything. We should tell our children it's all right to say no to any request from a dating partner that makes them feel uncomfortable or ashamed, or that is against gospel standards. Red flags to watch for in dating partners include the following: Clinginess, anger problems, controlling behavior, attempts to make the dating partner feel guilty or responsible for the abuser's feelings and actions, isolating the dating partner from family and friends, manifesting a big difference between words and actions, major mood swings, inability to listen to or respond to the word "no," threats, and constant put-downs.

SIBLING ABUSE

Abuse between siblings should not be ignored. It's our responsibility as parents to intervene immediately when one of our children abuses another. It is important to take the offending child away from the victim and describe the behavior that was not acceptable. It's also important not to use physical force or anger. While responding, it's helpful to use consistent and measured responses and then give the child time to think and talk about his or her actions and feelings. It's also helpful to have the child consider the feelings of the sibling who was hurt so they can develop sensitivity to other children. Appropriate consequences should follow, and an apology is also in order.

SIBLING SEXUAL ABUSE

If sexual abuse has occurred between siblings, intervention with a legal professional outside the family is necessary. The sexual abuse of younger children by an older sibling might be an indication that the older child has also been sexually abused. This cycle of victim being abuser dramatically supports the advisability of early, intensive intervention in child sexual-abuse cases in which juveniles are the offenders. Failure to report sexual abuse within the family compromises the offender's accountability and puts everyone at risk for further abuse. Incest usually requires that the perpetrator be removed from the home. In most cases, sexually abusive behavior will not stop without accountability and treatment for offenders.

Siblings of any age never have the right to abuse other siblings. It's important to put abusive adult siblings on notice that cruel behavior will not be tolerated. If necessary, brothers and sisters may have to remove themselves from their relationships temporarily or permanently. If safeguards and directives for respectful treatment are not honored, siblings who are abused by other adult family members should consider reporting cruel, harassing, or threatening behavior to their local law enforcement agency and obtaining court orders.

Many adults abuse their parents and siblings for years by demanding money or other assistance while they continue in abusive, illegal, or irresponsible behavior that puts their family members at risk. Ill-informed parents sometimes place pressure on their adult children to remain in a relationship with an abusive sibling in the name of family solidarity. Other well-intentioned but misguided family members think forgiveness means tolerating ongoing abuse. Being members of the same family does not give anyone the right to harm, threaten, or frighten.

ELDER ABUSE

When family members caring for an elderly relative abuse or neglect them, their behavior is referred to as elder abuse. Elder abuse includes all forms of abuse previously discussed and often also involves withholding food or medication, neglecting to bathe or toilet, taking the elder's possessions, and restricting contact with the outside world.

SPIRITUAL ABUSE

Spiritual abuse includes any attempt to control or dominate others (even for their own good). Christ influences us through selfless love, not by subjecting us to His will. When we believe and act as though we alone are right and everyone else must agree with us to be safe or in good standing with us, we are spiritually abusive. Spiritual abusers are so determined to defend their way of thinking or doing things that they abuse anyone who questions or disagrees with them or doesn't behave the way they want them to. Spiritual abusers use thought control, threats, deception, guilt trips, judgments, and holier-than-thou attitudes to control others.

Dominion is not acceptable for any reason and should not be part of any man or woman's influence. Dominating, diminishing, damaging, or destroying another person's spirit through religious scare tactics is spiritual abuse, as is threatening to publicly humiliate. Spiritual abuse includes acting in ways designed to make others feel inferior, diminished, subordinate, judged, preached to, unloved, and rejected. Spiritual abuse also includes using someone's religious beliefs to manipulate or ridicule them or making efforts to prevent them from practicing their beliefs.

Spiritual abuse includes personal elitism manifested by drawing on our private association with God or knowledge of doctrine to intimidate, show superiority over, control, induce guilt in, or dominate others. Spiritual abuse also includes using priesthood position, motherhood, self-proclaimed inspiration or revelation, and prophetic dreams or visions as a means to impress, intimidate, or silence differences of opinion. True spiritual power, potential and influence are based on personal sanctification not gender, position, or piousness.

The powers of heaven come to bear only when Christlike individuals refuse any power over those they love and seek to serve.

Spiritual abuse also occurs when someone assigns evil or sin where there is none, uses false accusations to destroy a reputation, or controlls others through deceit and fear. Spiritual abuse includes using sacred temple ceremonies or ordinances in word or action while committing any form of abuse.

God, who knows all and has all power, chooses not to use compulsion or dominion. Though it is appropriate for parents to set rules and teach correct principles, it is never necessary to manifest disrespect for a spouse, child, or sibling. Righteous relationships with a spouse, child, or sibling always include Christlike behavior. Those who understand the righteous use of influence never abuse others. Respect and trust are earned by consistently loving, gentle, and unselfish behavior.

Righteous influence is manifested when adults help children learn firsthand about consequences for behavior, help them develop mature decision-making skills based on gospel principles, and assist them in learning how to personally give heed to the guidance of the Holy Spirit. Righteous influence also includes loving and gentle teaching about how to access and accept the power of the Atonement to repent from mistakes, both our own and those of others. Righteous influence lifts, blesses, enlarges, expands, loves, and encourages.

Comments such as "I'll never be good enough" or "I'm not celestial material" are often used by people who were or are spiritually abused. Those who spiritually abuse usually think they are doing the "sinner" a favor by using guilt, shame, harsh punishments, and letter-of-the-law pronouncements in an attempt to correct or control behavior. But righteous influence never gives others a dark feeling about themselves or a damned prognosis about their eternal potential.

Ecclesiastical leaders can help those who abuse to repent. They can also provide kind, caring attention to members who have been abused. They can guide both the abused and the abuser along the path to repentance, forgiveness, and ultimate healing through the application of the teachings of Jesus Christ and the Atonement. They can assist members in finding competent professional and legal help. They can encourage members to seek God's help. But they can't solve family problems and shouldn't be asked to take sides or be used as threats.

Personal patterns of worship should not be used to intimidate or exert power over other members of our family. Praying, going to the temple, reading the scriptures, or forming any other personal worship habits help us be worthy to receive revelation about how we should be repenting and what we should be doing to better serve and love others. Personal inspiration does not give us the right to dominate or force others in the family to behave the way we desire. When we receive spiritual direction, we should keep that inspiration between us and God and then use our influence over others in loving and Christlike ways. In some cases, it may be appropriate for family members to share their inspirations, as long as they're not used to control.

Because the priesthood gives a man the right to preside over his family, some men mistakenly believe they have male privilege and the right to control or dominate their spouse and children. Some women also feel they have the right to control or dominate their husbands and children for their own good because they (the women) believe they are more in-tune spiritually. *Preside*, in fact, means to take responsibility for the well-being of family members by loving, serving, blessing, inspiring, and directing. In this manner, husbands and wives preside together. Men and women have equal access to all the gifts of the Spirit. Jesus Christ provided the perfect example of how to preside righteously. His condescension in our behalf and His submission to God was complete and far beyond our ability to understand or appreciate. He led by His totally unselfish and loving example.

The scriptures are clear about the righteous exercise of priesthood, and for that matter, any unrighteous use of authority by either man or woman. "The powers of heaven cannot be controlled nor handled only upon the principles of righteousness. That they may be conferred upon us, it is true; but when we undertake to cover our sins, or to gratify our pride, our vain ambition, or to exercise control or dominion or compulsion upon the souls of the children of men, in any degree of unrighteousness, behold, the heavens withdraw themselves; [and] the Spirit of the Lord is grieved" (D&C 121:36–37).

Even though women are not given priesthood responsibilities in this life, they have access to every gift of the Spirit. There is no difference between the spiritual power of men and women. Spiritual power is based on personal righteousness and our connection with God.

Those who spiritually abuse their families permit self-proclaimed personal righteousness to give them a sense of superiority. Spiritual abusers see their role as the person who must constantly call others to repentance. They feel driven to constantly put others in their place and point out their weaknesses and relish the role of expert on all spiritual matters. A spiritual abuser is hoarding a tremendous amount of anger because others don't do what the abuser wants them to do. He or she hides deep feelings of rage by use of condemning judgments and evaluations of others instead of careful self-purification. He or she insists on an authoritarian-punitive-vengeful method of punishment for crimes both real and imagined. People who spiritually abuse often claim to have revelations, dreams, inspiration, and clear impressions about what others need to be doing. Those who spiritually abuse their families have a need to find fault, convict, and sentence others for their misdeeds, both real and imagined. They do not understand that all change must start with self.

About the Author

Janene Baadsgaard has written extensively with warmth, valuable information, insight, and humor about family life for over thirty years. She is the author of hundreds of newspaper columns and features, many magazine articles, and over a dozen books. She is a graduate of Brigham Young University in Communications with a journalism emphasis and has taught courses in writing and literature for Utah Valley State College. A popular speaker, Janene has sharedher wit and wisdom with thousands at such events as BYU Education Week, BYU Family Expo, BYU Women's Conference, and Deseret Book's *Time Out for Women,* as well as at numerous other civic and church sponsored events. She is the mother of ten children and grandmother to many. She lives on two acres in Spanish Fork, Utah. Her hobbies include reading, writing, singing, playing the piano and violin, and gardening.

Some of her books titles include *Is There Life After Birth?, A Sense of Wonder, Why Does My Mother's Day Potted Plant Always Die?, On the Roller-Coaster Called Motherhood, Families Who Laugh . . . Last, Financial Freedom for LDS Families, Grin and Share It: Raising a Family With a Sense of Humor, Sister Bishop's Christmas Miracle, Expecting Joy, The LDS Mother's Almanac, Winter's Promise, Fifteen Secrets to a Happy Home,* and *For Every Mother.*